live

the moment

live

the moment

Paul Arnott

HarperCollins*Publishers*

HarperCollins*Religious*

An imprint of HarperCollins*Publishers*, Australia

First published in Australia in 2000
Reprinted in 2001, 2003
by Dove Communications Trust
Trading as HarperCollins*Religious*
ABN 20 348 975 034
A member of the HarperCollins*Publishers* (Australia) Pty Limited Group
www.harpercollins.com.au

HarperCollins*Publishers*

25 Ryde Road, Pymble, Sydney NSW 2073, Australia
31 View Road, Glenfield, Auckland 10, New Zealand
77–85 Fulham Palace Road, London W6 8JB, United Kingdom
Hazelton Lanes, 55 Avenue Road, Suite 2900, Toronto, Ontario M5R 3L2
and 1995 Markham Road, Scarborough, Ontario M1B 5M8, Canada
10 East 53rd Street, New York NY 10022, USA

Arnott, Paul
   Live the moment: The Ten Commandments of living for today.
   ISBN 1 86371 796 X
   1. Life skills. 2. Conduct of life. 3. Self-actualization (Psychology).
   I. Title.
158.1

Cover photograph: International Photographic Library
Cover design: Katie Mitchell, HarperCollins Design Studio
Printed in Australia by McPherson's Print Group on 79gsm Bulky Paperback White

7 6 5 4 3   03 04 05 06

CONTENTS

For Rosanne, my partner in the
challenge to live each moment to the full

My thanks to

John Waterhouse, for his friendship and his determination to help this book see the light of day; Tim Costello, for the inspiration of his life; Margaret Houston and Peter Grant, for their contributions to this project — they have influenced my thinking and writing more than they realise; Roslyn Hunt and Jo Stansall, for their many suggestions; Robyn Claydon, for her insight and feedback; my thanks to all at HarperCollins during the production of this book; Joanne Cornish; Pt Arthur survivor, Peter Crosswell; Camp Quality and the Banham family, for their willingness to share so openly their struggle in having a child with cancer; Dr Leon Morris, for the inspiration of his commentary on the Gospel of St Matthew; Bob and Pru Wakelin, for their many suggestions and encouragement; my parents, Laurel and Arthur, and my sister, Lindell, for their unconditional love.

In commenting on the brutal murders of thirty-five people at Port Arthur on the 28th of April 1996, I have avoided using the name of the person responsible. I do so because I am unwilling to give the gunman any more recognition than he has already received for the murders he committed.

particularly from what his children say to him. Whenever I speak it is the wisdom our children teach us that my audiences love best of all.

Perhaps we should take the author's advice and set our priorities in terms of what we really want so that we have time to listen to our children more often. How can we do this? I can only reply with Paul Arnott's wisdom. He tells us he suspects 'that the only way to live simpler lives is to want less'. It is profoundly counter-cultural advice, but I can recommend it.

Rev. Tim Costello
President, Baptist Union of Australia

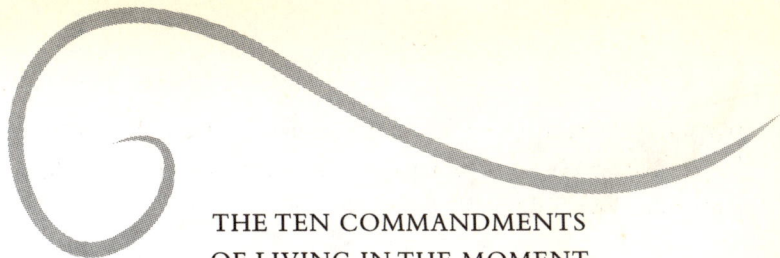

THE TEN COMMANDMENTS
OF LIVING IN THE MOMENT

1 Focus fully on each moment of every day.

2 Habitually tune in to the world around you.

3 Be emotionally, as well as physically, present for those you love.

4 Recognise that you have the power to choose how you react to others.

5 Cultivate the habit of forgiving those who hurt you.

6 Set your own agenda.

7 Make time to be still each day.

8 Accept that your worth is determined by who you are, not what you do.

9 Do not try to see into the future.

10 Face your own mortality.

INTRODUCTION

We need to learn to live more fully in the moment. If we don't we won't stay sane in the face of this increasingly complex, troublesome world of ours. We live in one of the most stressful times in the history of the human race. Life in the new millennium will create problems for us as individuals and as a planet of even greater complexity. Society, as we have known it since the Industrial Revolution, will continue to change.

One in every hundred sexually active adults on the planet now is HIV positive. Racial hatred has become an epidemic, with the obnoxious phrase 'ethnic cleansing' now used worldwide to justify genocide against religious and racial minorities. The lax handling of the nuclear arsenal and biological weapons by countries belonging to the former Soviet Union means we are still faced with the spectre of a global catastrophe. The destruction of our environment continues unchecked. Global warming and the destruction of the ozone layer will, if not remedied, cause the illness and deaths of thousands of human beings. Droughts caused by mismanagement of the Earth's resources are causing the deaths of millions in Africa and Asia. The over-prescription of antibiotics and their use to prevent disease in animals may see the emergence of pandemics that cause the deaths of millions of people because new bacteria have become antibiotic resistant. The most widespread fear among people today is fear about the future.

When, on the 28th of April 1996, a gunman brutally murdered thirty-five people at the historic tourist site of Port Arthur in south-eastern Tasmania we were forced to acknowledge what we had long suspected: life is no longer safe, not even in sleepy Tasmania. We came to see that if people can die suddenly and brutally on a peaceful Sunday afternoon while eating lunch and sipping tea, they can die anywhere at any time in any place.

Simply coping with the speed of change has become a daily challenge. We have information coming at us from every direction: via the TV, radio, post-box, newspapers and magazines, the Internet and computer software. We are in the middle of a technological revolution, which will change our lives as much as the Industrial Revolution changed the lives of the people of the eighteenth century.

Doctors are becoming aware of a new syndrome called Information Fatigue Syndrome, the symptoms of which include paralysis of analytical ability, mounting anxiety and self-doubt, and an increasing tendency to blame others. It is suggested that more than one-third of all reported stress-related illnesses are being caused by information overload. There is a famous scene in the media movie *Network* in which the lead character, a television presenter, screams out the window, 'I'm mad as hell and I'm not gonna take it any more.' More and more people feel like they can't take any more of life the way it is. Youth suicide in the eighteen to twenty-four year age group has reached epidemic proportions in many countries, because many of our young people see no hope for the future. People are more stressed, more pressured than ever before.

To live longer, to live more healthily and to live more fully we need to find new resources and skills to cope. Medical science is just beginning to realise that health is inextricably linked to lifestyle. Two hundred years ago people died from typhoid and diptheria. Now we die of the stress-related diseases of cancer and coronary heart disease.

Our frenetic lifestyles are making us sick, robbing us of the richness of our relationships with those we love, and killing us. I believe that one of the greatest causes of stress is the inability to live in the moment. We can find ourselves dwelling on the past with all its guilt and hurts, being traumatised by the future with its fears and anxieties, or living in the present in such a frenetic way that we fail to live life. Often we are just existing, instead of really living each moment to the full. The demands of daily life are so great and we are so busy that we constantly feel there isn't enough time.

On King Island off Tasmania's north-west coast, the wind is so strong that most of the trees have grown on an angle instead of straight. The elemental forces that have shaped them have caused them to grow abnormally, but the wind is so constant the effect has become permanent. The same can be true of life. The pressures of life can cause us to grow crooked, and out of balance, but to feel that crooked is normal. Learning to live in the moment will help us regain our balance. It's the way we've been designed to live.

CHAPTER ONE

The dilemma

When our second child, James, died of SIDS at the age of nine weeks, our lives were turned upside down. We experienced indescribable pain as the result of his death. But we also learned how to live one day at a time. We came to realise that life is a precious gift, which we must never take for granted. This is a corporate as well as an individual truth. Every day we live as a human race on this fragile planet, sailing through space, is a gift.

However, this is something we need to learn again and again. Even though we gained this insight as a couple through pain and tears, we can easily lose it in our busyness. Our experience has been that living too much in the past, too much in the future or too busily in the present robs us of life now.

An unexamined life is a wasted life. If all we do in life is to go round the sun seventy or so times on Planet Earth, eating, sleeping, working and trying to fit in a bit of pleasure here and there, then life is mere existence. Human beings need to live life deliberately, not by default.

Yet the death of our son was not the only thing that motivated me to live more fully in the moment. A few years ago my eldest daughter, Alice, used to play the Harry Chapin song, 'Cat's in the Cradle'. It begins with the father talking about his newborn son and his own busy life with not enough time to notice his child's important milestones. The little boy grows up quickly and tries hard to please his parents, especially by following in his father's footsteps.

Towards the end of the song the by-then retired father phones his son, trying to arrange a time for them to meet. The son is far too busy with his own life and his own family and so has no time for his father. The old man puts down the phone sadly realising he only has himself to blame for setting such a bad example of how to live.[1]

When I first heard 'Cat's In the Cradle' I made up my mind not to become like that father. I began to work much harder at making time to spend with my children in the moment. Children grow up very quickly. It seems like yesterday that our eldest was born and she's now fifteen and in Year Ten at high school. Our youngest has begun school and is growing fast.

THE RIDDLE OF TIME

From the beginning of recorded history, time and its passing have been a mystery to human beings. This very moment in which I write these words is the present for only a split second. The words I have just written are now the past and nothing I do can change that past. Nor can I change the future, over which I have no control. Not only is time a mystery, but it also creates anxiety — largely because it is beyond our control.

It's not only hurts from the past and fears about the future that rob us of life in the present, but also the way we live in the present. We live such frenetic lives. We cram our lives full of activity, but often our activity is just a running away from what is inside us.

In the words of former United Nations Secretary-General, Dag Hammarskjöld:

> When all becomes silent around you and you recoil in terror — see that your work has become a flight from suffering and responsibility, your unselfishness a thinly disguised masochism; hear throbbing within you, the spiteful cruel heart of the steppe-wolf — do not then anaesthetise yourself by once again calling up the shouts and horns of the hunt, but gaze steadfastly at the vision until you have plumbed its depths.[2]

We are afraid of the stillness of the moment. We're afraid that if we are quiet for too long, we may hear things we don't want to hear, we may have to deal with issues we have swept under the carpet. But we will grow as human beings only as we face these issues, 'plumb the depths of the vision', no matter how unsettling they may appear to be.

TAKING LIFE FOR GRANTED

A play, '*Our Town*' by Thornton Wilder, had a strong impact on me. It highlights the importance of not taking life for granted. The play tells the story of George and Emily who grow up together, fall in love and are married. Their married life begins well, but then disaster strikes — Emily dies in childbirth. However, in the story, she is given the opportunity, after her death, to go back and relive one day of her life. She chooses, despite the advice of the others buried in the cemetery, to go back to the small town of Grower's Corner where she grew up, for her twelfth birthday.

When she returns, she watches the events of that busy day begin to unfold. She sees the hustle and bustle, the wrapping of presents, the cooking of the birthday cake, the hanging of streamers and the blowing up of balloons. She also notices that, even though her family live in the same house, they hardly notice or know each other.

In the end, in desperation, she pleads with her mother to just look at her daughter for one minute as though she really saw her. She begs for just a moment of looking at one another and being together and being happy.

At the end of the day, she arrives back at the cemetery in tears to hear Simon Stimson, the deceased organist and town drunk, tell her that ignorance and blindness are what it's like to be alive. She wanted to go back to where people spend and waste time as though they were going to live for a million years.[3]

We can experience life but, in our preoccupation, miss its meaning. We get only one chance at life, despite what some people like to believe. If we squander this, there is no second chance on this Earth. Nothing is ours but time. In terms of the length of human history the span of one lifetime is the flicker of an eyelid. We have a responsibility to make the most of the time we have here. While everyone dies, not everyone really lives. Each day, each hour, each minute needs to be a new beginning. Every new morning we wake to a new day; every breath we take; every time we look into the face of someone we love are unique opportunities to make everything new.

OUR BONDAGE TO THE PAST

Another factor that causes people to fail to live in the moment is past hurts. This is especially true of grief. There is evidence that a great deal of mental illness stems from unresolved grief. Statistics show that as many as one-third of all patients visiting their local GP have problems that stem from unresolved grief. The old way of dealing with grief was to pretend the person had not died or that they hadn't even existed.

In tribal Aboriginal culture, this is still the case. If an Aboriginal person dies, their name is never used again. In Western culture, this has been a recipe for enormous internal conflict.

I once met a woman who gave birth to a stillborn baby in the 1940s. In those days when a child was stillborn it was covered with a sheet and quickly whisked away. Its parents never saw the baby. They didn't name it. They didn't even know what gender it had been. The wisdom of the day said that the best thing for parents was to get on with life as if nothing had ever happened.

The woman I spoke to had never spoken of her feelings about having a stillborn child to another human being until she spoke to me. This depth of hurt has crippled the lives of thousands of people all over the world. It has prevented people from living fully in the present because so much of their energy has gone into dealing with hurts from the past. There is also mounting evidence that a large number of people who have been sexually and physically abused as children live bitterly unhappy lives because of the past abuse.

Resentment and unforgiveness over past events can overshadow our lives and prevent us from being the people we were created to be. I have spoken to many, many people who have held on to grudges against someone over something that was done or said that hurt them deeply. Sometimes these hurts go back very many years. I have heard so many people say something like this, 'I can forgive most things, but I will never forgive that' and they will then go on to catalogue the particular offence against them. Mostly these people cannot see that the resentment is hurting them and affecting their lives far more than it is the life of the so-called guilty party. The resentment eats away at their ability to live life more fully in the moment.

Guilt is also something that can rob us of life in the present. We live in an age that tends to say guilt is both bad and unnecessary. But if we have done things we know were wrong, the way to deal with the guilt is not to sweep it under the carpet by rationalising what we've done, but to deal with guilt at its root — to face it and name it.

OUR PREOCCUPATION WITH THE FUTURE

As Western people, many of us tend to live in the future, both mentally and emotionally. We spend a great deal of time anticipating events: holidays, romantic dinners, retirement — a whole host of things, most of which are good and exciting. But the reality rarely lives up to the expectation.

Our desire to try to preserve our lives also locks us into the future. So much of our lives revolves around discussions about investments, insurance and superannuation. What is gambling all about if it's not looking to the future to hit the jackpot and solve all your problems? In tight economic times this is especially so. The irony is that in such times we can't afford to be pouring hard-earned cash into a poker machine.

Advertisers are constantly encouraging us to look forward to getting this device or gadget which 'we absolutely need' to make our lives easier. The reality is that such devices make our lives more complicated and cluttered. We can do more, but because we can do more we have less time and we are less able to live in and enjoy the moment, especially our relationships.

Computers are a good example. The microchip enables us to do things that twenty years ago were simply not possible. But because we are able to do these things we have less time and, because we have less time, we live less fully in the moment.

Our whole way of thinking locks us into dwelling on the future rather than the present. We're forever waiting for something to happen. A writer I admire, Henri Nouwen, suggests that 'the real enemies of life are all our oughts and ifs. They pull us backward into the unalterable past and forward into the unpredictable future. But real life takes place in the here and now.'[4]

The future is a place of fear and the unknown, which is perpetuated by the mass media. The media exaggerates our fears, especially television news, which sensationalises and trivialises. So much of our daily news focuses on fear of the future, world starvation, economic collapse, renegade nuclear threat, political instability and war.

Our lives can become consumed by fears about the future. What if I lose my job, what if my loved ones die, what if there is not enough money, what if the economy collapses, what if a third World War breaks out? The future can be a frightening place, especially if we let our imaginations run riot. We can spend a great deal of time worrying about what may or may not happen. However, few people sink under the weight of the day. It's when we add anxiety about tomorrow to the burden of this day that life seems out of control.

We are not meant to live in the future. We're designed to live in the present. Henri Nouwen writes, 'These many "ifs" can so fill our minds that we become blind to the flowers in the garden and the smiling children on the streets or deaf to the grateful voice of a friend.'[5]

OUR OVER-BUSYNESS IN THE PRESENT

If the past and the future conspire to rob us of life in the moment, so too does the busyness of the present. I have a poster of two birds sitting on snow-covered trees in the depth of winter which says, 'What is life, if full of care, we have no time to sit and stare.' We are victims of time in a society that is constantly worried by the passing of time. We are constantly checking our watches and looking at clocks. Time controls our every moment.

Try not looking at your watch for an hour or, better still, take your watch off for a day! You quickly discover the grip that time has on our lives. Men, especially, are slaves to time. The men's movement has revealed the extent to which men are workaholics. Men are fiercely competitive with each other — something bred into us from an early age. Not only do they constantly compete with others, they compete with themselves. Those who are baby boomers especially are locked into the desire to make a significant contribution to the world they live in. They are very ambitious, but the problem is the more they want to achieve the less time they have, which means they have to work even harder to get it all done.

In a recent article on two best-selling real estate managers, one stated his aim in life was to fit as much into his life as possible, while the other said his greatest dislike was lack of quality time with his family. Life in the moment is so busy most of us never have the space to enjoy the living we're doing. Many women will attest to having partners who are physically present but emotionally absent. Often at home I know I can be physically present but mentally absent. My mind is on the busyness of the day or the day to come and I'm just not 'with' my family. This can have a devastating effect on both our partner and, if we have them, our children.

I was concerned to read a recent Morgan and Banks survey of mid-level to senior business people which showed that 52 per cent were so unhappy they intended to look for other jobs almost immediately. One employee in three worked more than forty hours a week, while one in five worked more than fifty hours a week. Studies show that people with full-time jobs are now working so hard that their overtime absorbs another potential half a million jobs. Ten years ago, 29.3 per cent of Australian employees worked more than forty hours a week. By 1997, the figure had risen to 31.9 per cent. More than half the business people in Australia believe they are overworked and want new jobs.[6]

Busyness has become an end in itself, a justification of human existence. However, so much energy goes into coping with the stress of simply living from day to day that we don't have time to deal with the big issues of life.

An example of our hectic, stressful lifestyle is my friend, who is thirty-four. He has an upper-middle management job in a growing Australian company. But he has found over the past three years that he has had to work harder and harder just to stay on top of his work. He writes:

> I'm finding it a real struggle. I enjoy my job, but I'm working seventy hours a week. The pressure is on because I'm well paid and I know there's a queue behind me a kilometre long. I rarely see the kids. When I leave for work, they're only just getting out of bed and when I get home they're almost in bed. Sundays, which should be a break, are just work days at home. My wife and I seem like strangers. Our conversation is nuts and bolts stuff, like school fees and paying bills. I don't want it like this, but I don't know how to change it. The scary thing is that I can't see it getting any less busy.[7]

There are very many people in the same position. Life in the present is just so busy there is no time to reflect or think or feel. All our energy goes into living. While many Australians believe they are overworked, one million Australians are living with what is probably an even greater stress — the inability to get a job. In a society that values what people do more than the quality of their character, there are few things more debilitating than long-term unemployment.

If our attitude to time is flawed, then all we are and hope to become, along with everyone and everything we touch, will also be flawed. Somebody once said that when we're stressed out, we need to sit under a gum tree until we're bored. This is great in theory, but sometimes we can feel so stressed that the thought of sitting still for more than a few moments creates more, not less, stress. We need to learn how to restructure our lives in a way that enables us to live more fully in the moment — to learn to treat each moment as precious, to savour it, to fully experience it and to make the most of it.

LOOKING FOR REAL LIFE

When I first read sociologist Tony Campolo's book *Carpe Diem*, I identified very strongly with what he was saying. He tells about asking participants attending one of his seminars the question, 'How long have you lived?' When no-one answered, he chose a young man in the front row and asked him, 'How long have you lived?' He blurted out: 'Twenty four years'.

'No,' Campolo said, 'I didn't ask you how long you've existed as a member of the human race. I wanted you to tell me how long you have been really alive.'

When all he got was a blank look, Campolo told the story of his visit to New York when he was twelve. Standing on top of the Empire State Building for the first time, he experienced a moment of 'heightened awareness, a hyper-intensive consciousness, far too wonderful to describe. In a mystical way I stepped outside myself at that moment and reflected upon myself experiencing it'.

Campolo told his student: 'I do not know how long I will live, but if I were to live a million years, I would remember that moment because I truly lived it.' Then he asked again: 'How long have you lived?' The young man thought for a long time before saying: 'When you talk about living like you lived that particular moment in New York, maybe a minute. Maybe two. I mean, if I were to add up all those times when I experienced life with that kind of heightened awareness, they're not likely to come out to much more than that'. He then added regretfully:

'When I stop to think about it, most of my life has been the meaningless passage of time between all too few moments when I have really been alive.'[8]

SEARCHING FOR ECSTASY

When I first read this story, I thought, 'Yes, Tony Campolo is right; so much of our lives can seem like the meaningless passage of time.' We need to find more moments when we really live. I searched my memory for moments when I had truly lived.

I remembered looking out the window of the bus taking me into Athens and seeing the Parthenon for the first time, my first experience of an overseas country. I remembered standing at the foot of Big Ben in London and thinking, 'This isn't a film or a picture in a book. This is the real thing.' I remembered standing on a cliff on the Dingle peninsula on the west coast of Ireland at dusk, overwhelmed by the beauty of that ancient land.

My experiences of overwhelming awareness of the present moment during my travels were special. But I remembered, too, one mellow, warm morning in childhood on a family holiday at the beach in Tasmania when I woke to sunlight pouring in the window, the smell of pine cones, the familiar call of a magpie, sand in the sheets and the crisp, fresh feel of a new day.

ECSTASY V AWARENESS

My 'aha' experience in Tasmania is the moment described by many poets, a moment that seems super-real. Poet Clive Sansom writes of one such moment in his experience, during the Second World War, in Austria:

> *There are moments —*
> *So intense, so beautiful —*
> *They pierce through space,*
> *And hang poised forever*
> *Beyond the clutch of time.*[9]

But as I reflected on these 'aha' moments, I realised that, while they were experiences of living in the moment, what was really being described were moments of ecstasy. We could spend the whole of our lives searching for such moments of ecstasy. Indeed, some people do — sexually or spiritually.

However, searching for moments of ecstasy is very different from learning to live more fully in the moment. Living in the moment is about becoming aware of each moment as it is lived. It is about feeling the wind blowing on your face, smelling freshly ground coffee, taking the time to notice the colour of the eyes of the person you're talking to, making time to listen to the story of your child's day at school. It is about noticing the beauty of creation in a sunset or sunrise. It is about smelling rubbish at the tip or feeling the freezing wind off snow on a mountain. It's not simply a search for pleasure and enjoyment.

It's living all that life brings our way, as fully as possible. It's about being alive. Moments that seem quite ordinary can come alive when we focus our full attention on living this moment in time. This moment now as I write these words, this moment as you read these words, is unique. There will never be another moment like it. As we discover how to live each moment fully instead of having our attention elsewhere, we will find that each moment can be special. It may well be that what we call 'aha' moments are rare only because we live so much of our lives with our attention elsewhere. When we begin to live more fully in the present, we will discover a richness of living that we didn't think possible.

EVERY MOMENT IS PRECIOUS

Life goes so fast. When our first child, Alice, was born, a wise friend with adult children said, 'Enjoy your children. Make the most of them because they'll be gone before you know it.' After our son died, we were overwhelmed not only by the fragility of life — if he could die unexpectedly, so could any other of our children and so could we. We were also overcome by a sense of the wonder of each new day. Each day was a precious gift that should never be taken for granted. Every moment was a gift from God to be lived as fully as possible.

In my first book, *No Time To Say Goodbye*, I recorded this comment by Catherine, whose four-year-old daughter was accidentally hanged:

> I remember wandering aimlessly for hours on the beach and along the country back-roads near our home. One morning, I got up at dawn and walked along the beach. It was one of those clear beautiful blue-skied mornings —

not a cloud in the sky and so still. There was a seagull flying so high it was almost out of sight ... I remember being overwhelmed by the realisation of what a precious gift life is, that every moment of every day is to be treasured and savoured because we never know how long we'll have it.[10]

When our son died I began to realise in a unique way how precious life is. I described life as a gift. However, I have come to see that rather than life being a gift it's really on loan to us from God. What we have, who we are and who we will become isn't totally in our control. I believe life's experiences drive this home to us all the time. Life is not under our control. There is fragility about life, which people in Australia have been made aware of in tragic ways in recent years. The killing of thirty-five people at Port Arthur and the tragic loss of nineteen people at Thredbo have driven home to us the reality that none of us is guaranteed life. This is a fact of which people in two-thirds of the world are only too aware. For them, death on a massive scale is a daily event — in Africa, Asia and South America.

To make the most of life, we need to live it to the full by living in the moment. Life can be so much more than 'the meaningless passage of time'. And yet living in the moment is one of the hardest things any human being can attempt to do. We shouldn't need tragedy in our lives like the death of a loved one or being told we have a terminal disease to help us to learn not to take life for granted. We can learn it now. That's what this book is about — learning how to better live in the moment.

At a glance

We have only one shot at life,
so we must make the most of it.

Don't take life for granted;
learn to live fully in the moment.

Don't dwell on past guilts and future worries —
they can rob us of life now.

CHAPTER TWO

People who have learned to live in the moment

When I was younger I used to believe that life was meant to be essentially problem free. I was overly idealistic: 'We were put here on Earth to be happy, and problems and disappointments were aberrations not to be tolerated.' But I soon discovered that life isn't like that. Life is full of problems and griefs and disappointments. The secret is to find positive ways of responding to the problems life brings us daily that enable us to live life to the full. One of the best sources is to look at the wisdom of the past and the lives of those who have gone before.

Not surprisingly, as the quintessential teacher on the human condition, Jesus Christ had a great deal to say about the best way for human beings to live. He suggests that one of the keys is to live in the moment. His teaching in the unsurpassed Sermon on the Mount gives us some great insights:

Therefore I tell you, do not worry about your life. Don't worry about what you will eat or drink; or about your body, what you will wear. Is not life more important than food or clothing? Look at the birds in the sky. They don't plant or harvest; they don't even store grain in barns. Yet your heavenly Father feeds them. Aren't you worth more than birds? Can worry make you live longer? Why worry about clothes? Look how the wildflowers grow. They don't work hard to make their clothes. But King Solomon with all his wealth wasn't as well dressed as one of them. God gives such beauty to everything that grows in the fields, even though it is here today and thrown into the fire tomorrow. He will do even more for you! Why do you have such little faith? Don't worry about yourselves, 'Will we have anything to eat? Will we have anything to drink? Will we have any clothes to wear?' Only people who don't know God spend their time worrying about such things. Your Father in heaven knows about all your material needs. But, more than anything else put God's work first and do what he wants. Then all your material needs will be met. So do not worry about tomorrow; tomorrow will worry about itself. You have enough to worry about today.

(Matthew 6, verses 25 to 34).[11]

COPING WITH ANXIETY

Jesus says anxiety achieves nothing. In fact, it is totally counter-productive. Worry can literally make us sick. Anxiety is a major factor in a number of diseases, including hypertension, stomach ulcers and cancer.

Jesus gives a number of sensible reasons for trusting God instead of worrying. He sees a lifelong habit of entrusting ourselves to God as the secret of life. If God is really God, can't God be trusted with every detail of our lives? For if God is God, everything about us is known. There is no hope or hurt, dream or disappointment secret to God.

My maternal grandmother Alice used to tell the story of a man walking along a dusty country road, staggering under the weight of a large sack of potatoes. A farmer offered him a lift, which he gratefully accepted. After a while, the farmer noticed the man was still carrying the potatoes on his shoulder. 'It's alright,' he said. 'You can put them down.'

'Oh no,' the man replied, 'I couldn't expect you to carry my bag of potatoes as well as me.' We laugh at the simple-mindedness of the potato-bag carrier, but so often this is how we respond to God. We feel we don't have the right to burden God with our worries. We feel that God is far too busy managing major international global crises to possibly have time to care for our needs.

WE CAN LEARN FROM CREATION

In the Sermon on the Mount, Jesus uses creation to teach us how to trust God more fully.

'Look at the birds,' he says. 'They teach us a great deal about trusting God. Birds don't sow or reap crops, but that doesn't mean they starve. Nor are they idle. Is there anything busier than a sparrow? They build nests and search for food and care for their young.'[12]

Jesus' point is that, although the birds don't sow, reap or store away in barns, they are fed. 'Your heavenly Father,' he says, 'in whom the anxious have ceased to trust, provides even for the happy-go-lucky birds.' Jesus says that we are much more valuable than any number of birds, so what makes us think that our Father won't also care for all our needs?[13]

Jesus is so often seen as a very serious-minded person in the Bible, but here we find him displaying a sense of humour. He asks his disciples which of them can grow taller by being anxious? You can almost hear the amusement in his voice. His point is simple. No matter how much we worry we can't make ourselves any taller. The Greek word for height here can also mean age, so Jesus may be asking, 'Will worrying make you live longer?'[14] The answer is obvious.

Anxiety does nothing, except rob us of life in the present. We know from hard experience that worry achieves nothing positive. It can lock us into a permanent state of anxiety and can even make us sick. The one thing it doesn't do is add to the quality of our lives. Sometimes we can even worry about not having anything to worry about! Jesus says we're not to worry about either the future or the past, because it will achieve nothing. Then he turns his attention to clothing. He says if God looks after the grass of the fields, which is here one day and gone the next, how much more will we be cared for? So, Jesus says, don't be anxious about food or drink or clothing. God knows what we need and will provide for all our needs.[15]

PUT WHAT IS MOST IMPORTANT FIRST

Then Jesus spells out a principle which, if put it into practice, will enable us to live in the present more effectively than anything else I know. He says that we are to steep ourselves in God's reality, to seek first God's 'kingdom and righteousness' before anything else.[16]

So many of us spend our lives trying to meet our own needs first. But that is putting the cart before the horse. We have been designed to have a relationship with God at the very centre of our lives. Every human being has a God-shaped space in their lives. When we fill that space with

God and seek to live our lives the right way, everything else will fall into place. But if we spend our lives trying to fill them up only with the material, the temporal, leaving God out of the picture, we will find that nothing will ever fully satisfy us. Jesus rocked that perception when he declared that, when we put God at the centre, all our material needs as well as our spiritual ones will be provided for.

HARD-HEADEDNESS KILLS WORRY

Jesus is often portrayed as a mystical, almost dreamy-eyed teacher, but there is a sharp-edged practicality about him. He says, 'Don't be anxious about tomorrow. For tomorrow will be anxious about itself'.[17]

What did he mean? Was this an early form of the power of mind over matter: that if we do not worry about something, it will simply go away? Was Jesus an early advocate of the power of positive thinking? Or was he advocating some sort of paradigm shift, encouraging people in some sort of way to look outside the box? Whatever, Jesus boldly declared that there is no need to be anxious even about tomorrow, let alone about the days and weeks after that. This was another way of saying that worry should always be put off.

There is a scene in *Gone With The Wind* when Scarlet O'Hara, who has shot and killed a soldier who attacked her, says, 'No, I'm not going to think about it now. I'll worry about it tomorrow!' This is the kind of attitude we all need to develop in regard to worry. Tomorrow's worry is never a worry if we postpone it until tomorrow because 'tomorrow never comes.' If worry is confined to 'tomorrow', we are free of it, because it is always 'today'.[18]

Jesus finishes by saying, 'Today's trouble is enough for today.' Once again, there is a note of ironic humour. We instinctively know this to be true. How many days are trouble free? Yet we are rarely anxious about today. It's the future that bothers us. If we restrict our worrying to today, we defeat anxiety. Jesus is saying there is the world of difference between reacting to the problems of life with anxiety and fear and facing them with firm faith in a God who loves us.

In my experience, there is nothing that will more surely rob us of life in the moment than anxiety about the future. For many years I allowed anxiety about the future to rob my life of the richness of the present moment. It sapped my enjoyment and caused me to be permanently distracted. Of course, the irony is that 99 per cent of the things we worry about never happen. But, then, it's too late. The moment has come and gone.

THE SECRET OF CONTENTMENT

Very few people I know are content with what they have. This is certainly true of money, but it's true of other aspects of our lives as well — health, work and career, educational opportunities, even body image and physical appearance! Over the years, I've asked a number of hairdressers how many people are happy with their hair the way it is! Their answer is always the same: very few people are happy with the hair they have. If someone has straight hair, they want it to be curly or wavy — and often are prepared to spend a great deal of money making it that way. If someone has wavy or curly hair, they invariably want straight hair If it's blonde, they want to be brunette, if it's thick they want it to be fine — and so the list goes on. The old adage 'The grass always looks greener on the other side' is true of almost every area of our lives. There is wisdom in being content with what we have.

Someone who was always content with whatever he had was the apostle Paul. Paul, or Saul as he was then called, was a vehement opponent of Christianity, but, following an encounter with Christ on the road to Damascus, became its greatest proponent. Paul learned to be content with his circumstances no matter what they were. He was arrested a number of times, beaten up, imprisoned and, on several occasions, almost murdered. But he had learned the secret of contentment. He was able to live contentedly in the moment, free of past guilts and future anxieties, because he knew his life was in God's keeping. On one occasion, he and a man called Silas were in prison for teaching people about Christianity. It was about midnight and, despite the extreme discomforts of prison, he and Silas were singing hymns. Hymn singing has never been a common activity in prisons. It wasn't then and still isn't today. Paul writes:

> I have learned to get along happily, whether I have much or little. I know how to live on almost nothing or with everything. I have learned the secret of contentment in

every situation, whether I have a full stomach or whether I'm hungry, whether I have much or little; for I can do everything God asks me to do with the help of Christ, who gives me strength and power.

(Philippians 4, verses 11 to 13).[19]

STRUGGLING WITH MYSTERY

After my son James died, I struggled to understand why. I had looked forward to the birth of a son so much. I realised some months after James' death that I would never teach him to play cricket, something I had always imagined I would do if I had a son. It seemed so unfair that after only nine weeks this beautiful little boy, loved so greatly by his sister and parents, should be dead. As parents we would have died in his place had we been given the opportunity.

History and life are full of injustices. Ironically some of the most horrendous events of history took place in the so-called enlightened twentieth century – the two World Wars, the Holocaust, the genocide in Cambodia, Rwanda and Bosnia. While I don't understand why God allowed these terrible tragedies to happen I have come to see that I don't have to subject God to my standards. Certainly, it doesn't seem fair that my son died before he had had a chance to live. But it wasn't fair that Jesus died when he was only thirty, that Madeline and Allanah Mikac died at Port Arthur with so much life ahead of them, that six million Jews died under the Nazis — or twelve million White Russians. That millons died in Cambodia, Rwanda and Bosnia. Or that Raoul Wallenberg, who saved the lives of thousands of Jews during the Holocaust, should be falsely imprisoned by the former Soviet Union.

I've realised that God is not subject to my judgement. God's ways are higher than my ways and God's thoughts higher than mine (Isaiah 55). It may just be that on a day to come, the things that don't make sense now will make sense then because we see more clearly.

Ultimately, I trust that the things that now make no sense will, in the end, prove to be part of God's loving purpose for our lives. Certainly, it is this trust that enables me to live more fully in the moment.

LIVING A DAY AT A TIME

Australian writer on spirituality Margaret Houston is someone who has learned to live in the present moment. Margaret, one of the most wonderful people I know, has learned what many of us have half discerned but never fully comprehended — that living in the moment is not only about moments of ecstasy; it is also about ordinary moments, even painful ones.

When I asked her for some thoughts on the subject,[20] she told me that for her, living the moment was linked inseparably to her faith in God, which she describes more as a love affair than the attempt to obey a set of rules. She begins by quoting 'C.S. Lewis' from the play *Shadowlands*: 'No, I don't want to be somewhere else any more, not waiting for anything new to happen, not looking round the next corner or over the next hill. Here and now — that's enough.'

Margaret adds:

All lovers know that the presence of the beloved is enough. So, for me, now is enough — sitting at this table, drinking this cup of coffee, staring at this view, struggling with this piece of writing, aching with this strained neck muscle. Enough because deep down somewhere inside, outside, wherever, I know I am in communion, communicating with him.

This moment is like most of my moments: ordinary, banal, routine. But being with a lover, human or divine, transforms everything, making even the tedium bearable.
In the play, C.S. Lewis also says, 'Experience is a brutal teacher — but you learn, by God, you learn." Experience has been my brutal teacher. Loving truth means that I see the present moment as it really is. Without God, the present moment is futile, however beautiful my thoughts, however lovely the flowers and mellifluous the sound of birds. Life without the One who created it is pointless, dreary, empty, meaningless — and terrifying.

Fear and boredom drove me into the arms of God. He was a last refuge from disappointment. I read Brother Lawrence and Thomas Kelly with longing. They seemed to have found some deep contentment, some inner peace in a way that didn't seem to have made them super-spiritual sentimental saints. I discovered from them that God is there to be found, just as we grow up hoping to find that special someone 'across a crowded room', who turns out to be just another human being in need of love, food and clean socks!

Imperceptibly, I have begun to live. Living isn't boring, but it isn't comfortable either. More changes, more challenges, becoming more like Christ. At the moment, I live in the moment because, in my relationship with God, it is the only time in which I have the physical energy, emotional capacity and inner resourcefulness I need. In other words, I only receive grace to live as God wants me to live in this present moment.

Some people discover how to live in the moment as the result of tragedy and trauma. Among this group are those who have had to cope with terminal disease in their own lives or the lives of those they love. There are also those who have lived through great human tragedy like the ethnic cleansings of Bosnia and Rwanda, or survived appalling massacres like the one at Port Arthur. Such people discover that life is precious, that every day is a gift, that every new sunrise is special.

JO'S STORY

Jo Cornish is someone who has learned how to live better in the moment as the result of trauma in her own life. Her father, Don, died in 1990 after a twenty-year struggle with multiple sclerosis. Then, six weeks after finishing her term as Miss Australia, she went to the doctor when she had trouble breathing. Tests pinpointed five lumps in her chest and on her lungs. Jo was told it was 99 per cent certain that she had Hodgkin's disease, a rare and life-threatening cancer. She takes up the story:[21]

> I went through so many different emotions in forty-eight hours. From complete denial to throwing full-scale tantrums. I felt 'This isn't fair. I've done nothing in my life. Haven't I already had enough bad things happen to me? It's someone else's turn.' I experienced all these thoughts and feelings during the first night.
>
> Then I clicked into what I call secretarial mode. I realised I couldn't change it. There was nothing I could do. It was completely out of control. It was almost like being conquered. I thought: 'There's nothing I can do to change it. I'll just have to roll with it,' which is exactly what I did.

From then on in it was a bit robotic. I went into hospital and spent most of my time making sure Mum had lunch and letting friends know. I couldn't change it, so I made up my mind to refuse to think about it. I'd felt so alive before because I'd had so many exciting things happening to me that my initial reaction was one of self-pity. It just seemed so unfair.

However after three days of tests doctors discovered that what had appeared to be cancer was in fact not. The disease Jo had was treatable and not life-threatening. Initially, she was furious:

I wasn't angry that they told me it was cancer and then discovered it wasn't. I was angry because I had lain in the hospital for three days planning exactly what I would need to do to get through this. I had worked out in minute detail schedules for getting to and from the hospital for chemotherapy to fit in with my work with Southern Cross Television. I had worked out everything to do with my job and my family, even down to a trip to the hairdresser to find out how to strengthen the roots in my hair to minimise hair fall-out. I'd gone through everything.

Suddenly it dawned on me that, while my meticulous plans for the next year had been undone, I didn't have cancer. And then I fell asleep for about three hours! The exhaustion had caught up with me.

Jo says that these experiences have helped her to live life more fully in the present:

As I looked back at my childhood — the fact that Dad was always sick and then had to go into an institution, that Mum chose to go to Iraq to live — I thought nothing else could possibly go wrong for me because I had served my years of hurting. The rest of life had to be wonderful. Then when I was told I probably had cancer, I realised that hurts happen all the time and you can't count on life being wonderful just because you've had a few knocks.

I feel that I've grown stronger as a result of these experiences. I guess, too, I came to realise that I wasn't invincible. I think I thought I was, but this experience has taught me that I need to look after my body more and take care of it. I am learning to treasure every moment, every day, every friendship, every thought that you have because — at any second — it can be snapped away from you so quickly. I don't ever want to be in that situation again and have things I need to say to people or need to do and have to make rush phone calls before I go under the knife.

Jo says:

I was just so angry that my mum decided to go and live in Iraq twelve months after Dad died. I wanted her to sit in Launceston, grow old and be bored, but be there on the odd occasion I needed her. That's what mums are supposed to do, not flit off to the other side of the world to places that seem very dangerous from our Western perspective. Because she went, I made up my mind never to allow myself to need her again. I didn't want to have to rely on her and need her as a mum or as a friend.

Yet when I went into hospital, she was the only person I wanted to be there. I realised that, while we play these mind games, we do need our families. I came to see that I will always need her and had to stop being selfish in wanting her to be here for me and have no life of her own while I got on with living my life. I saw that even though I had to let her go I would always need her and want her. Our relationship has been quite different since then.

SARAH BANHAM

Paul and Jane Banham will never forget Christmas 1993.[22] Their eleven-year-old daughter Sarah got sick five days before Christmas Day. She was vomiting and had a high temperature so her parents took her to the local after-hours doctor, who suggested that her stomach pain possibly indicated a bowel virus. The next morning the family GP confirmed the likely diagnosis and told the family to bring Sarah back if she hadn't improved by Christmas Eve.

By Christmas Eve, she had stopped vomiting, her temperature had gone down and she slept most of the day. However, four days later she still hadn't picked up, so her parents took her back to the doctor. When he examined her, the doctor discovered she had an enlarged spleen and sent her off for an ultra-sound. This showed that Sarah had a tumour. The surgery to remove the tumour revealed that it was an aggressive type of cancer that required radical radiation and chemotherapy treatment. She then had to undergo ten weeks of chemotherapy and eighteen days of radiation treatment.

Paul and Jane were shocked by the news that Sarah had a tumour. Their shock only deepened when they discovered it was an aggressive cancer that required such radical treatment. The hardest thing for them was watching their daughter in pain as the treatment was given. Following fifteen months of treatment, a scan picked up another tumour. The long operation to remove the second tumour was followed by three days of chemotherapy in Melbourne and over a week of blood transfusions in isolation.

Jane and Paul have a very real faith in God and through this time were aware of people's prayers. Paul said that his faith had grown as a result of all that had happened to Sarah:

> Initially I felt God was a bit of a spoil-sport and I didn't really want to find out what he wanted for my life. I prayed from Day One: 'God, Sarah is in your hands. Whatever way you want it to go.' I remember holding her a few moments after she was born and praying that God would take care of her. I have continued to pray that all the way down the line.

When I spoke to the Banhams they had just received the news that Sarah's cancer was back and the prognosis was not good. Did this change the way Paul was feeling?

No it didn't. He simply told God, 'Well, she's in your hands. We'd prefer to have her alive and well if that is possible. But whatever happens, she's in your hands.'

Jane said she had recently been given a plaque of the poem 'Footprints'.

> I know that in the next few months I will have the opportunity to put into practice the truth of that poem — to let God carry me and us as a family through this time. I used to pray for parking spots. Now my prayer is that Sarah won't suffer, a prayer which the doctors say should be answered with the wonderful palliative care that is available these days to people in pain. I also know that because God is our Father, he will understand that we will need a bit of time and that [after Sarah dies] we're not mad at him and still love him.

Jane says she has learned a great deal through this experience:

> During Sarah's illness, people would say, 'Oh, but she's your only daughter!' However, my attitude is that we've got a daughter. There are people who have no daughters, maybe no children at all. There are people who didn't

have their children for nearly as long as we've had Sarah. We've been thankful for what we've had.

In recent times, we've made an effort to do more things together as a family. We went camping together for the first time as a family and that was great. If I work a weekend, Paul will take the children roller-blading or on the bike track — things that even a few years ago we couldn't do because Christopher was too small. We haven't spoilt our children with money or things but with time. We've tried to be with them at sport and school much more. We're there for them much more than we used to be.

Paul and Jane talked openly with Sarah about the fact that it was quite likely that she was going to die. Sarah was able to say that she wasn't worried about dying. They also told Sarah's brothers, Phillip and Christopher, it was very likely their sister would die. As a result, the likelihood that Sarah would die became part of family conversations and they would hear the boys say to Sarah, 'Well, when you get to heaven, you'll be able to do this or that ...'

Sarah Banham died at home in July 1996.

PETER CROSSWELL

Few Australians will be unaware of what happened at Port Arthur on the afternoon of Sunday 28th of April 1996. It is a tragedy that has been forever engraved into the psyche of the people of Tasmania. The murder of thirty-five unsuspecting people in such a violent manner was something that shocked and scared the nation, indeed the world. Since then many people have found themselves asking, 'If this kind of senseless massacre can happen in a place like Tasmania, can it not happen anywhere, at any time, to anyone?'

Peter Crosswell was at Port Arthur on the 28th of April 1996.[23] Peter is the State Manager of Camp Quality, an organisation which runs a camping and support program for children with cancer. He had planned to take his whole family to Port Arthur that day, but providentially, one by one, they found other things to do and in the end he took with him only two visiting Camp Quality puppeteers. When they arrived at the Port Arthur Historic Site they decided to have a cup of coffee and something to eat in the Broad Arrow Cafe. Peter said that just after they sat down in the front section of the cafe there was a series of loud bangs in the back section of the cafe. One of the puppeteers suggested that it must be a historic re-enactment. However, Peter said that Port Arthur didn't have that sort of re-enactment and that it must be something exploding in the kitchen. When the bangs continued Peter Crosswell recognised them for what they were — gunshots. The gunman had systematically shot dead a number of people having lunch in the cafe. Peter Crosswell says the casual, methodical way in which they were shot is forever engraved on his memory. He recalls:

> I remember a number of people running towards me because I was between them and the door. The two puppeteers were sitting ducks as they had not grasped what was happening, so I grabbed them, pushed them to the ground and lay on top of them.

Peter says he told them to stay still, but one of the women lifted her head to see what was happening and was shot. Fortunately, while the bullet knocked her hat off, the only damage it did was to graze the left side of her head.

Peter Crosswell said they lay there for what seemed like ten minutes. He was later to discover that it was only one minute and fifteen seconds, during which time twenty people died. He says that he was absolutely terrified and convinced that he was about to die. A person lying on the floor next to him (not one of the puppeteers) was shot in the head:

> He stepped over my legs on his way to kill people in the souvenir shop. During the shooting I was wounded by shrapnel. Fortunately though, it was only a flesh wound and while it was very painful it didn't do a great deal of permanent damage.

Peter says that while he was initially terrified after a while he experienced a tremendous feeling of calmness:

> It was an extraordinary experience. I'm sure I felt calm because I accepted that I was going to die. I remember feeling an overwhelming regret that I would not have the chance to say goodbye to my wife and children and wondering how they would cope.

Since that terrible day in April 1996 Peter Crosswell has changed a great deal as a person. However, not all the changes have been for the better. While he and his wife grew far closer to begin with, two years ago his marriage broke down, largely as a result of the stresses caused by the events of the 28th of April. But he says that having had to deal with the shock and grief caused by the massacre has helped him empathise with the families he works with whose children have cancer: 'I can see parallels between what I've experienced and all they are going through as families struggling to come to terms with having a child with cancer.'

I remember the same feeling at the national SIDS conference Rosanne and I attended in Brisbane the year after James died. At the end of a talk, the man I was sitting next to, who had also had a child die in cot death, and I just put our arms around each other and wept. There is such a solidarity in being with others who have experienced the deaths of children. Also, they seem to share a similar worldview, as they now know, as we do, that children can die and that the world will no longer be the safe place it had once been.

Peter Crosswell takes life less for granted now than he did before:

I find myself making more time to do the things I really want to do. Before I used to say 'Oh, I must go trout fishing', but wouldn't get around to making it happen, but now I do it because I discovered on 28th April 1996 that tomorrow doesn't always come. Work has also changed for me. I'm a lot more focused and my productivity has increased.

Peter says that there isn't one day that goes by without him thinking about Port Arthur and how his life has changed since then:

It was a real breakthrough to accept that Port Arthur has become part of my life. The horrible memories of that day are a burden I bear and no matter how much I'd like to change what happened I can't. But accepting that has helped me to move on. I don't get scared anymore in the way I used to.

Profound suffering affects people in profound ways. We do no justice to belittle that suffering or try to put a pious gloss on it. Rather, by facing it head-on realistically, truthfully, we are better able to come to terms with the horror of what we have experienced and what we have become. Only then can the rebuilding of our shattered lives take place. Peter Crosswell says:

> There are some things I can't do any more like using a rifle to hunt. But life goes on. I'm far more aware of life as I'm living each moment. In fact I'm excited about the rest of my life. I feel that I have a lot more control of my life and where it's headed and that's a good feeling. I guess more than ever I want to make a difference and I can see a way of doing that through my work with Camp Quality by caring for families in crisis.

FRANCOIS' STORY

One of the wonderful things about living in Tasmania, the friendliest and most beautiful place in the world, is that we have a steady stream of international visitors. Last year I met one such visitor by the name of Francois. He turned up at the parish office looking for a place to stay — for one or two nights, he said. However, one or two nights blew out into several weeks and we got to know Francois quite well. He told me that he had been travelling the world for twenty years. He would travel until his money ran out, then find a job and earn enough money to continue his travels. Francois said it was uncanny how whenever he needed work he found it.

He told me about an experience he had when climbing Mt Kenya in Africa which demonstrates wonderfully the importance of living the moment. He had been warned that all sorts of robbers made climbing the mountain quite dangerous but he did it anyway. On his way back down he met two very shady looking characters. One of the men was the most evil looking person he has ever met. They told him they wanted everything he had. I asked him what he did: 'I gave them everything they wanted because I was convinced that if I did not I would be a dead man.' They took his backpack and all his clothes except his shorts. They even took his boots. Francois said that as he walked back down Mt Kenya, semi-naked, he experienced an overwhelming sense of gratitude that he was alive. He said that the loss of virtually everything he owned helped him to discover what really mattered — that even if he lost all he had materially, life would still go on and he would still have relationships with those he knew the world over.

At a glance
We must tune in to the world around us,
to experience all our senses fully.

Living each moment at a time helps us to
live less anxiously.

Tragedy in life can make us more aware of its
fragility and preciousness.

CHAPTER THREE

Dealing with the past

DEALING WITH PAST HURTS

I have met so many people whose lives are hampered, sometimes even crippled, by hurts from the past. Hurtful and damaging experiences can leave us with remembered and lingering emotional responses that limit our freedom to live life as intended and prevent us from experiencing God's grace fully.

I need to say here that I approach this whole area of healing past hurts within the context of the Hebrew-Christian tradition. I have seen God bring resolution and healing to past hurts in the lives of very many people, including my own. It is not enough to say, as some people have, 'I'll just ignore the hurts of the past. If I pretend they didn't happen, they won't have any influence on me.' To adopt such an approach to past hurts is to be locked into denial. All the evidence indicates that our past experiences have an enormous influence on our lives in the present.

In his book *Inner Healing*, T.E. Dobson describes the characteristics frequently found in people needing inner healing:

> The burden of pain that all of us carry drains our energy from creative and productive activity and makes us feel unworthy, guilty, hopeless, broken and unforgivable. This burden would be destructive enough if its effects went no further, but such is not the case. These negative feelings, now converted over a period of time into attitudes, begin to develop within us negative patterns of behaviour, and our past begins to destroy our present. That which is so negative begins to want to destroy itself and so we develop habits of self-destruction or habits of sin.[24]

Hurts from the past affect our lives in the present. Often these hurts are so deep, they can rob us of quality of life here and now. So much emotional energy can be going into dealing with the hurts from the past that there isn't much left for living in the present. Sometimes, people can appear to be coping with life, but beneath the surface it's a different story. Like the swan sailing serenely along on the lake while beneath the surface of the water it is paddling for all it's worth, so in my experience many people are serene on the surface but 'work like crazy' just to stay afloat.

THE PAST HAS SHAPED US

We are all products of our past experience. What has shaped us more than anything else, as marriage educators have known for many years, is our experience of our family of origin. The greatest influence on our lives is our experience of the family in which we grew up (we will examine this later in this chapter).

We are, to a very large extent, a product of that family environment. So it is crucial that we deal with past hurts and guilts. This doesn't mean that the events that are causing us hurt will automatically change when we face them.

However, sometimes, simply facing the past honestly and being able to bring our hurts and griefs out into the open is enough to break their power over us. But if the hurt has been a deep one, just becoming aware of it, even beginning to understand it, will not necessarily break its power over your life in the present. There are no quick cures for deep hurts.

A USEFUL MODEL

Dennis and Matthew Linn, in their book *Healing Life's Hurts*, provide a useful model to help understand the process of healing pain from the past. They base their model on Elizabeth Kubler-Ross' five stages that dying people go through: denial, anger, bargaining, depression and acceptance. Kubler-Ross sees these five stages as the normal way of healing any deep hurt. The Linns suggest that in seeking healing of past hurts people usually go through those same five stages as shown in the table on the following page.[25]

Five stages in the process of healing

Stages		People's reactions in the process of facing mortality or in healing past hurts
1st	**Denial**	People struggle to admit they will ever die or that they were ever hurt
2nd	**Anger**	People blame others for letting death destroy them or blame others for hurting and destroying them
3rd	**Bargaining**	People set up conditions to be fulfilled before they are ready to die or they set up conditions to be fulfilled before they are ready to forgive
4th	**Depression**	People blame themselves for letting death destroy them or they blame themselves for letting hurt destroy them
5th	**Acceptance**	People make the change so that they look forward to dying or they make the change so that they look forward to growth from hurt

QUALITY OF LIFE

The euthanasia debate, which has generated such emotional heat in the community, has raised the legitimate question of the quality of life in the cases of people with terminal disease. The proponents point out a self-evident truth: that simply because a person lives a long life does not guarantee that he or she will live a rich and fulfilling one. Many people are tormented by past hurts to the extent that life in the moment is unpleasant and sometimes unbearable. Past hurts, especially as a result of childhood sexual abuse, can cause the victims to feel that life is not worth living.

In the end, what makes life worth living isn't its length, but the way we live our lives. For life to be worth living, it must have purpose and meaning. There are people who have lived for only a short period of time, but have lived full lives because their lives have had meaning and fulfilment. They are, I believe, people who have learned at an early age how to live the moment.

MY OWN EXPERIENCE OF THE
HEALING OF PAST HURTS

I have experienced three specific instances of healing from childhood hurts. The first event happened when I was a small baby. I don't remember it because I was only a few months old, but I was told about it on numerous occasions in later childhood.

To say I misbehaved as a kid is probably an understatement. I know my parents would defend my childhood record and point out that really I was just a lively little boy with lots of energy. But I know what I was like.

My mother has told me that when I was a very small baby and I was crying with some passion on a visit to the baby health clinic, the clinic sister looked at me and said very sternly, 'Stop bullying your mother!' She then pronounced, 'This child will always have to learn the hard way.' She may well have been right anyway, but as I was told about this prediction on a reasonably regular basis, it became for me a self-fulfilling prophecy. The nursing sister had said I would always have to learn the hard way in life and I set about to prove that she was right.

It was only in adulthood that I realised that what she had pronounced over me at such a tender age helped to lock me in to always having to learn the hard way. Sometimes in my late teens, I was aware that there was an easier way, but as I was a young man who 'always had to learn the hard way' I'd better do it the hard way. Now I look back and realise what grief I could have saved myself and others by taking an easier way, but then it seemed that the hard way was the only one I knew. This is a tendency I struggle with even today. I don't believe these words *caused* me to have to always learn the hard way. All the nurse did was to accurately diagnose the problem. But rather than suggesting how my parents might help me change, she locked me into it.

As an adult, I came to see that this prediction had become a self-fulfilling prophecy in my life, something from which I needed to be set free. That release and healing came through, first, becoming aware that I was locking myself into doing things the hard way, even in adulthood, and second, through prayer for healing in a program called Prayer Counselling. This is based on the premise that we can be freed from the oppression of past hurts through the healing power of Jesus. I was freed from the impact of that prediction on my life.

The last two incidents that caused the hurts both occurred when I was about ten years old. The first happened when we were on holiday at a resort south of Hobart called South Arm. It was then, and still is, a superb holiday destination with beautiful beaches for families to enjoy.

We were staying at a holiday cottage. My sister and I fought a lot, like many siblings with only a year and a half difference in age. We loved each other and now in adulthood are very close, but we expressed our affection for each other in childhood by regular arguments. They were mostly verbal, but sometimes got physical. On this particular day, we were arguing over who would sleep in the top bunk. The top bunk was always the most prized position. The person in the bottom bunk could feel quite claustrophobic and anyway there was a moral superiority about being in the top bed. The argument quickly escalated into a physical affair and I pushed my sister off the top bunk onto the floor below. She fell about five feet and landed on her back.

At the time, I felt she was putting it on just to get sympathy and of course to make me pay for what I'd done, but I realised that she could have hurt herself really badly. Fortunately, she didn't do any permanent damage, although having all the wind knocked out of her was painful enough — plus the added indignity of being pushed off the top bunk. I remember watching her lying there and thinking, 'Oh, I'm really going to get it from Dad!' And of course I did. He was justifiably furious and in his anger blurted out, 'I'll kill you if your sister has really hurt herself.'

Deep down I knew that I deserved to be punished. I can't remember whether I got the strap, the standard method of punishment for any major misdemeanour in the Arnott household. But I do remember the words my father spoke. I know that he regretted them the moment they passed his lips and I know he felt bad about having lost his temper. But I have never forgotten those eleven words, even though God's healing has taken the sting out of them.

Whoever coined the phrase 'Sticks and stones may break my bones, but words will never harm me' didn't live in the real world. Words hurt a great deal, especially if they're words of anger from someone we love. Those words etched themselves into my memory. I knew my father loved me, but the words were a shock. I knew it was really his anger speaking, but the words and the anger behind them hurt. I wish I could say that my experience meant that I never uttered similarly angry words to my children, but I can't.

FACING THE PAST

The other incident happened shortly afterwards. My mother was gardening in our backyard in the Hobart suburb of Mount Stuart when she stood on a rusty nail. When she went to the doctor, she was given a precautionary tetanus injection, which caused an anaphylactic reaction, which we realised later could have killed her. She experienced an extreme allergic reaction which later caused her to swell up and she had difficulty in breathing. She was rushed to hospital and, as a result of the allergic reaction, suffered a mental breakdown. Mum went into hospital care for three months. My sister and I were told the bare details, but didn't fully understand what had happened to our mother.

It wasn't until I received prayer and counselling that I realised what impact this event had had on my life. As God was asked to bring healing of past hurts in my life, I was suddenly overwhelmed with a feeling of grief at what had happened. All the memories came flooding back, including the feeling of having been deserted. I guess three months in the life of a ten-year-old boy who was very close to his mother was a long, long time, especially when I didn't really understand why Mum had gone away.

As the prayer session continued, I entered into the experience of that ten-year-old Paul and sobbed, 'Mum, Mum, why did you go away when I needed you so much? Why weren't you there when I needed you?' I was a young boy again, grieving over being separated from his mother. I don't understand how all this happened. Some people would call it psychotherapy, although there was no probing, no questioning about my experiences when I was ten years old. God simply pinpointed the experience behind the hurt and brought it out into the open.

I experienced an overwhelming awareness of God's presence with me and all the sting was taken out of the experience. In the case of my father's anger over the bunk incident, I experienced similar healing. I was able to forgive my dad and be released from the hurt of those angry words. I also saw more clearly than ever before that my security is in God as my heavenly Father. I am able to bring all my worries and concerns to God and know they will be carried for me. I can leave my problems with God and know that everything will work out in the end, even if it doesn't seem fixable at present.

I guess ultimately that's what faith in Christ is all about for me. It's entrusting to God the whole of my life — my loved ones, my future, my past and my present. It's allowing God to be at the very centre of my life and living my life according to priorities, laid out in Scripture, that God has determined for my life.

THE HEALING POWER OF LOVE

Simply becoming aware of past hurts is not enough to bring healing. The actual hurt, which is with us in the present and prevents us from living fully now, has to be dealt with. Also the healing may take time. It can happen instantly and I have certainly seen that happen, but more often than not the healing takes place over time. The hurts have come about over a long period and the healing of those hurts takes time, too. There is often a need for what former Roman Catholic priest Francis MacNutt calls 'soaking prayer':

> Soaking prayer conveys the idea of time to let something seep through to the core of something dry that needs to be revived. That's the way it is with the laying on of hands when we feel that God is asking us to take time to irradiate the sickness with his power and love. It is a very gentle prayer.[26]

One of the keys to receiving healing from the hurts of the past is to come to the place of knowing we are loved. When I worked as a journalist with the ABC, I once interviewed a man called Nigel Goodwin who had established a centre for Christians involved in the arts in Britain. I remember very little of the interview except one comment which had an enormous impact on me and which I have never forgotten. In fact, it has become something of a touchstone for me.

Nigel said: 'I am loved and, because I am loved, everything is all right.' He knew he was loved by God, his wife and his family. In that there was a great deal of security. It wasn't just the words he spoke; it was the peace and contentment with which he spoke that had such an impact on me.

There is great security in being loved. There is nothing more important in life than giving and receiving love. Mother Teresa once said that we will be judged on one thing and one thing alone: whether or not we have lived lives of selfless love. Certainly the Bible makes it clear that God loves all human beings, whether or not they are believers. In my experience, though, most people, including a number of church people, don't really know that God loves them as they are and that he wants an intimate relationship with them. Somehow, we feel that we have to earn God's love. But God isn't like that. We are all loved by God from the moment of our conception. Psalm 139 contains these amazing words and they apply to every human being on the face of the Earth:

> For you created my inmost being; you knit me together in my mother's womb. I praise you because I am fearfully and wonderfully made; your works are wonderful, I know that full well. My frame was not hidden from you when I was

made in the secret place. When I was woven together in the depths of the earth, your eyes saw my unformed body. All the days ordained for me were written in your book before one of them came to be.

(Psalm 139, verses 13 to 16).[27]

FEAR IS THE OPPOSITE OF LOVE

Some people believe the opposite of love is hate, but it is really fear. When we allow it, fear controls our lives. It saps our energy and takes away the joy of life. We live in an age of unprecedented fear. As we adjust to life in the twenty-first century, it is likely that there will be a massive increase in the fears people experience. The society we have known for the past four hundred years is rapidly changing — some would say disintegrating. The world no longer seems a safe place.

In his book *Do Not Be Afraid*, Michael Buckley tells the story of Brenda, who came to him for help:

For as long as I can remember, I never got any joy out of life and I have no happy memories of my childhood. My parents never showed me any real affection. I suppose that is why I could never make friends with anyone. They said I was a loner, but in fact I just felt worthless in myself. No one wanted to be my friend.

I suppose I should have made the effort, but I was afraid of rejection. My brothers and sisters seemed to be able to do everything. They were achievers. I achieved nothing. The other children teased me unmercifully, but that was better than being ignored.

I hated the playground because I couldn't join in their laughter or games. I spent recreation time in the toilet. When I left school, things went from bad to worse. I hated the job I got and was constantly off work. Finally, I lost the job and was soon on the shuttle between the doctor and the psychiatrist. My parents died. My brothers and sisters, who had all married by then, had given up on me. I know what depression is. What I had to live with was more destructive and painful than any form of depression.[28]

Then when Brenda was at her lowest ebb a person from the local church told her about a healing service. The woman picked her up and took her to the service. If she hadn't been given a lift there, Brenda says, she wouldn't have gone. Michael Buckley told her:

> God is your Father and you are special to him. Never mind what others think. You love yourself because you are unique. God your Father believes in you. You need to learn to believe in yourself.[29]

Brenda said that for the first time in her life she felt special to someone, and the tears began to flow. She just couldn't control them. She said she didn't know whether they were tears of joy or self-pity. All she knew was that she was being released from the prison she had made of her life. Over a period of many months her life began to change.

> It was a slow process, but it was worth it. Now, for me, after all these years of self-torture, life is just beginning. I never look back to the past any more. I can't change what has happened. I am free to help others who feel unloved and useless, because I have been down that dark and dreary path myself. My life has a purpose. I hope that I am a more joyful person than I was because I now know that life is really worth living![30]

PAST HURTS CAN EVEN MAKE US SICK

There is a great deal of evidence to support the assertion that hurts from the past, if not dealt with, can even make us physically sick. Canon Jim Glennon, the founder of Sydney's St Andrew's Cathedral healing ministry, says his experience suggests that up to 70 per cent of all physical illness has its origin in emotional factors.

Jungian analyst John Sanford's story of the mother of a young woman who died tragically in a car crash. As it was a one-car crash, there was the possibility of it having been suicide, which was very disturbing to her parents:

> Her body was horribly mangled and the catastrophe could hardly have been more unsettling. Her father wept over the death of his daughter and insisted on viewing her body, saying that until he did it would not be real to him. His grief was deep, but he bore the pain of it. Her mother did not shed one tear. She kept saying she believed it was 'God's will to take her to heaven.' She kept a stiff upper lip. Two years after the burial of her daughter the mother was also buried, dead from cancer. As her husband stood by the grave-side he confided in John Sanford, 'You know,

if my wife had only wept when my daughter died, she would not be dead now.'[31]

This does not, of course, mean that everyone who fails to grieve properly the death of a loved one will die of cancer, but it does seem that at least certain types of cancer may be induced by a repression of strong emotions like grief or resentment. We need to let out our feelings of grief in whatever way is most appropriate for us at the time of the hurt. It doesn't matter how we express them as long as we get them out into the open, rather than holding them in.

ABUSE IN CHILDHOOD

The hurts of childhood, with which we have lived for many years, will not just go away because we become aware of them. This is especially true of sexual and physical abuse in childhood. Most people who have been sexually and physically abused as children live bitterly unhappy lives because of past abuse. There is evidence that many inmates of prisons have been abused as children. A link has been established between sexual abuse in childhood and alcoholism and drug use in adulthood.

Cathy Ann Matthews, who was sexually and emotionally abused as a child, visited a large Australian women's prison. As she spoke to a group of sixty women prisoners about the hope for ongoing recovery, more and more women became visibly upset by what she was sharing about her own abuse as a child:

> As I spoke, several of the prisoners began to dig each other in the ribs like kids playing up in school. Then they became openly upset and gradually sauntered or tip-toed out, alone or in groups. By the time I'd finished, there were only about fifteen prisoners left and a few officers. It was obvious that I had stirred up a hornet's nest, but I wasn't sure exactly what was going on. I began to apologise to the head prisoner, but she said, 'Oh, it's not you. We're happy with you. The women are upset because they're remembering their own abuse and there's no-one in prison to help them.'[32]

FAILED FAMILIES

Hurt adults are almost always the product of hurt, dysfunctional families. In the same way that hurt people hurt others, hurt families hurt those who belong to them. Many parents are too busy or too preoccupied to give their children the time and closeness they need.

This is especially true of Australian society, in which 60 per cent of married women work. In many families both partners need to work simply to pay the mortgage or to ensure their children get a good education. Many relationships fail because the only time couples see each other is in bed, when mostly they're too tired to do anything except exchange a few exhausted words.

We live in the age of the absent father. There are whole generations of children who have not known the love and the parenting of a father, because even if the fathers have been physically present they are emotionally absent. As therapist Mary Pytches has pointed out in her book *Yesterday's Child*, communication is not something that just happens. It has to be worked at and is a two-way affair:

Communication is about giving the other person space to share their opinions, thoughts and feelings, in an accepting way. Many parents never make the effort to listen to their children. A child that doesn't feel listened to doesn't feel valued and a child who is not valued quickly becomes a hurt child.[33]

CHILDREN DEPRIVED OF AFFECTION

Many parents don't give their children the physical affection they need to be emotionally healthy. A great many older people were brought up to believe that once a child reached the age of four they didn't need physical affection. You might spoil them if you gave them too many cuddles.

This was especially true of fathers and sons. It was socially acceptable to cuddle and hug a son until he was three, but from then on shaking hands was the acceptable societal norm. I suspect this attitude originated in the reign of the emotionally repressed Queen Victoria, and somehow we've never quite managed to break free from it, which is tragic because it has done a great deal of damage to families.

Touching is so important to the healthy development of human beings. It is at the very top of our hierarchy of emotional needs. The story is told of an orphaned baby girl who was failing to thrive. The hospital staff were regularly bottle feeding her and changing her, but she was not growing. In fact, she was losing weight and the staff were afraid she would die.

Then one of the nursing staff decided to give the little girl a cuddle before putting her back down every time she fed her. The result was that the child began to rapidly put on weight. In fact, she soon became the healthiest baby on the ward.

THE CONSEQUENCES OF DYSFUNCTIONAL FAMILY LIFE

Children are survivors and will adapt in order to survive in a dysfunctional home. This may cause them to repress their feelings, to change their behaviour and even to deceive themselves with lies. The unconscious aim of such behaviour is always to minimise the pain and to provide protection against further pain.

Mary Pytches says that although these defence mechanisms may initially enable the child to cope, there comes a time when they are no longer necessary. Unfortunately, by that time they have become habitual, appear normal and are therefore very hard to change. She quotes Dr Charles Whitfield, who suggests that,

> Children from troubled or dysfunctional families grow up not knowing what is normal, healthy or appropriate. Having no other reference point on which to test reality they think their family and their life is the "way it is," with all its inconsistency, trauma and suffering.[34]

Mary Pytches tells the story of Susan, a single woman in her early forties. For most of Susan's childhood her mother and father had a strained relationship. Their marriage ended in divorce when she was only eleven. Not only was there very little communication in the family, but as a result of the divorce she was separated from one parent and experienced a severe disruption in the love process during her adolescence.

She finally asked for help when her anxiety totally overwhelmed her. She lived in constant fear of conflict and dread of loss. Two of the many irrational beliefs she held were 'I must avoid conflict at all costs' and 'I am responsible for everyone else's happiness'. These beliefs enabled her to avoid situations that had, in the past, caused her a great deal of pain and fear. However, the price she paid for this avoidance technique was continual anxiety and a list of unresolved issues with friends and family, which crippled her emotionally and prevented her from enjoying life in the present.[35]

Mary Pytches identifies a number of steps to help people break free from the damaging effects of past hurts.

First identify our losses or traumas

Only when we have identified the hurt can we begin to re-experience it. We have to go through our grief work and complete it. It is not useful to try to go around it or try to avoid it. As you work through these issues it is important to have a counsellor or therapist's help.

It would not be wise to try to do it on your own, especially if sexual abuse issues are involved, as the depth and hurt of the pain can be so great that it can be overwhelming and even lead to people feeling suicidal. You must not go it alone but must find an experienced person who can help you through these issues.

Next take time to grieve for lost parts of our childhood

Sometimes a person in depression is mistakenly thought to be in mourning. However, mourning has to happen separately. Depression can take a person close to their wounds, but only mourning for lost innocence can lead to people finding real and lasting healing.

Keep a diary or journal

One of the best ways to heal childhood hurts is to write a brief description of your family in your diary or journal. Just use one adjective for each family member such as 'My mother was kind (or bad-tempered). My father was loving (or bitter).'

You can also describe in your diary any known interruption to the love process. For example, I could write about the time when I was ten and my mother went into hospital.

Allow ourselves to grieve over loss in childhood

This can be a loss of a relationship, of joy in being a child or a loss of innocence.

Then, finally, close your eyes and imagine Jesus reaching out his hands towards you. He is bringing a gift for you. He is smiling as he offers it to you and you reach out to take it. The present he's bringing you is the beginning of healing in your heart.[36]

CREATIVE IMAGINATION

The practice of using the human imagination to create a picture of the way we believe God wants things to be is something that has been practised in the Hebrew/Christian tradition for centuries. In one parish in which I served, there were several extremely difficult people I had to meet with on a regular basis. I would have avoided these meetings if it had been at all possible, but it was not. These people seemed to go out of their way to make life difficult for me and would regularly verbally attack me.

After a few months of being pounded into the dirt every time we met, I began to use the process of visualisation in preparation for our meetings. I believed that God wanted these people to be at peace with themselves and others, even me. So I would spend the journey in the car on the way to the meeting imagining their faces in my mind. I would see them full of peace and speaking gently and nicely. I had to do this in a disciplined way, as it was quite easy to imagine them the way they had been, angry and aggressive and out to get me. But I forced myself to imagine them the way I believed God wanted them to be.

Every time I did this little exercise it had a major influence on the tone of the meeting. They were invariably much more polite and considerate. This practice can be applied to a wide range of situations. I have seen God use this many times to bring healing of past hurts.

MY FRIEND THE BURGLAR

Francis MacNutt tells the story of a woman who came to him with a very intense and completely irrational fear of the dark. As he prayed with her and for her, she was taken back in her mind to a time when she had been asleep in bed as a young girl. Before she had gone to sleep a burglar had broken in through her bedroom window and hidden under her bed. He may well have broken in and hidden under the bed when he heard her coming. He waited until she went to sleep and then tried to get out of her room, but she woke up and, hardly surprisingly, began to scream.

Her screams brought her parents running in panic. When he saw what had happened, the girl's father grabbed the hapless burglar and began to beat him up. This made the girl even more afraid. The entire incident was imprinted on her memory in a very traumatic way. Since then she had had trouble sleeping because of her fear of the dark.

Francis MacNutt then suggested that she imagine herself back into the original situation. There was silence for some moments as she did this and then she began to laugh. When he asked her what had happened, she said that she had relived the scene of her waking up, but that when she had woken up Jesus was there and that he had taken her hand and had introduced her to the burglar. Then when the parents had come into the room, he had introduced the burglar to them as well. The effect of this exercise was that all the fear was removed from the original experience. As a result, for the first time in twenty years this woman began to sleep peacefully, with no fear of the dark.[37]

HEALING GUILT

Guilt is one of the most destructive emotions we can ever experience. I have heard of many cases of older women who had had children out of wedlock, in an age when it was not socially acceptable to keep a baby unless you were married, and had had them adopted, who experienced guilt that ruined their lives. I have heard of many other women who have experienced enormous guilt as a result of decisions to abort unborn babies. Unfortunately most people who have been sexually abused as children experience a great deal of guilt. Many feel that it was their fault that they were abused. Often the perpetrator works hard to make the victim feel that what has happened is their fault. This is a way of controlling them and attempting to ensure their silence.

I once knew a woman in her seventies who had a so-called illegitimate baby. Her family had punished her severely for 'being such a bad girl'. And she had suffered so much guilt that she became mentally unwell. Sadly, she never came to see that self-forgiveness was the only way she could overcome the guilt, which was destroying her life. If we don't forgive ourselves, then we can't forgive anyone else. If we want to be healed of the hurt we've caused others or the hurt they've inflicted on us, then it is forgiveness that is the key to wholeness.

As we magnify guilt, we minimise forgiveness. God's forgiveness is always available to us, if only we will ask for it.

THE POWER TO CHOOSE

One of the most liberating things for any human being to realise is that they can choose how they want to react to the circumstances of life. We all have our choices, no matter how terribly life appears to have treated us. We are able to choose how we will react to what life brings. Some people believe they are not able to choose how to react. They just react. They choose to be victims rather than choosing to respond positively.

My late father-in-law, Clem Kent, demonstrated the truth of this principle very powerfully in his own life. Clem was captured by the Japanese on the island of East Timor in 1942, along with the rest of the all-Tasmanian Second Fortieth Division.

In fact, he was the person who decoded the semaphore message relaying the news that the Japanese had arrived. He then spent three and a half years in Changi. He experienced the brutality of many of the Japanese guards. He had many of his mates die after being sent to Thailand to build the Burma Railway. He saw friends beaten to death and executed. He saw close friends starve to death because there wasn't enough food to eat. But he never became bitter or hated the Japanese for what they did. Many Allied soldiers ended up hating the Japanese and wouldn't have anything to do with Japanese people.

CHOOSING NOT TO HATE

But Clem knew he could choose not to hate. I can still hear him saying, 'The average Japanese soldier was OK. Some of them were even kind to us.' I don't know how accurate a picture that is of the Japanese guards at Changi. Maybe he was being charitable. But what I do know is that he chose not to hate when he could very easily have hated. I believe that he made the right choice.

If we choose to hate, we are giving the person we hate

power over us. They are determining how we react. But if we are truly free, we will realise that we have the power to respond in a way that doesn't prolong the cycle of violence. Violence only begets violence. If somebody hurts us and we hurt them back then we make matters worse not better. It is only when a person responds to hate with love that life is transformed.

Jesus' response on the cross to those who wanted him dead is the most powerful example of this principle at work, 'Father forgive them for they don't know what they are doing' (Luke 23, verse 34).[38] Jesus chose to love and forgive rather than hating and, in so doing, removed all the sting from their hatred. We, too, have the freedom to choose to forgive rather than to react in resentment or hatred.

WE ARE RESPONSIBLE FOR OUR OWN LEARNING

That we are responsible for our own learning is something it took me many years to realise. Many people travel through life feeling that the odds are against them. But we can always learn from situations, no matter how bad they are.

My first boss was one of the most irritating, rude people I have ever met. He would stand next to me and drum his fingers on the desk while I worked, a habit which, as you might imagine, didn't exactly aid my powers of concentration. I spent the first six months of my working life reacting to this treatment: 'It isn't fair. People like this should not be allowed to supervise staff. How can any responsible employer expect staff to work under such conditions?'

However, in the end I came to see that all my reacting was achieving nothing. In fact, it was totally counter-productive. I began to hate the thought of going to work. I realised I needed to change my attitude towards this person. I began to try to see his good points. I saw his impatience as an opportunity to develop more patience myself. I tucked away for future reference a number of habits and work practices that I would never inflict on any staff under my supervision.

Many people have never discovered they have the power to choose how to respond to life. It has been said there is nothing we can do about what life dishes us up, but there is everything we can do about the way we respond. One of the hardest things about the Port Arthur massacre was watching the pain and hurt of those who survived and the families of those who died. Some were silent, others let it out. One mother whose teenage daughter died at Port Arthur said the gunman responsible 'should rot in hell.' It was an understandable emotion, but not conducive to her own peace of mind.

CHOOSING NOT TO HATE

What took place at Port Arthur on the 28th of April 1996 was something with which Tasmanians are still trying to come to terms. I, like all Tasmanians, will never forget that afternoon and the absolute disbelief, shock and horror as the grisly tale began to be told.

But what would be even more tragic would be if the events of that day at Port Arthur claimed more victims in the years to come as a result of people's responses to what happened. Some of the survivors are aware of this danger.

Some years ago I was part of a workplace morning tea conversation about a young girl who had been brutally murdered. There was a rumour that the girl's father had taken out a contract on the life of the man accused of having killed her. Almost everyone at the morning tea table that day, except me, felt that the father would be justified in having this man killed. I argued that this path would lead only to more violence. Look at Bosnia and Northern Ireland and Rwanda. Violence begets violence. The more people hate the worse things become. But, I have to say the only response to my comments was anger: 'How would I feel if it had been my daughter?' I don't know how I'd feel if a child of mine was murdered, but I hope that I would not choose the path of revenge. I know from hard experience that hating only makes things worse. Forgiveness not revenge is the way to health.

However, some people following tragedy are not able to get on with their lives. Some people feel overwhelmed by hatred and bitterness towards those who harmed them or their loved ones. If such emotions are allowed to become central to our lives, they can take us over and become very destructive forces.

DEALING WITH RESENTMENT

There is nothing more destructive of human relationships than resentment. I have met people who have held grudges against others for half a century, which have eaten away at them and even made them physically ill. The traditional Christian position is that we must forgive. However, while it is true that we should all forgive, people shouldn't be made to feel they should forgive without having worked through their hurts. As Dan Allender points out in *The Wounded Heart*, a book about healing childhood sexual abuse:

> Far too often the abused person is commanded to do good or to love their abuser without exploring the complexities of what it means to love or what may be blocking the God-given desire to love. The result is often a greater deadening of the soul in order to accomplish the burdensome task or a backlash of rage towards God or anyone who would so insensitively encourage such a painful path.[39]

However, people should forgive because they want to, not because they feel they're being forced to. Stephanie

Dowrick, in her best-selling *Forgiveness and Other Acts of Love*, lists some of the practical benefits of forgiveness. While this could make forgiveness sound like a selfish act, she is right:

> The muscular tensions you had come to assume were normal are eased. You are less vulnerable to infection or to far more serious illness. Your immune system lifts. Your face muscles let down. Food tastes better. The world looks better. Depression radically diminishes. You are more available to other people and a great deal more available to yourself, yet you think about yourself less and less anxiously.[40]

Of course, forgiveness is never easy, especially in situations of abuse. Forgiveness doesn't come naturally to us. In fact, Stephanie Dowrick asserts:

> Forgiveness deeply offends the rational mind. When someone has hurt us, wounded us, abused us; when someone has stolen peace of mind or safety from us; when someone has harmed or taken the life of someone we love; or when someone has simply misunderstood or offended us, there is no reason why we should let that offence go.[41]

I used to think forgiveness was something we did when people hurt us. But I have come to see in recent years that forgiveness is an attitude. Indeed it is a way of responding to life and to those who hurt us. Forgiveness is at the heart of Jesus' teaching and it is one of the keys to healing past hurts. By rejecting another person and refusing to forgive we are refusing to accept that we are part of the problem of unforgiveness. Refusal to forgive causes us to more deeply repress our own weaknesses. Ruth Carter-Stapleton has this insight into the dangers of such a course of action:

> Whatever we cannot forgive we are doomed one day to live. The reason for this is that the inability to forgive a frailty in another reveals that we are similarly flawed. If we had forgiven that weakness in another the act of forgiveness would have acted as an antidote to our own weakness. But our unwillingness to forgive fertilises the seed of that ugly quality within us.[42]

The words of the Lord's Prayer give us a better understanding of this issue. When Jesus tells us that we are to pray, 'Forgive us our sins, as we forgive those who sin against us,' he is saying that as we forgive others our hearts will be more open to receive God's forgiveness. Many people who have struggled with unrelenting guilts and fears need only forgive those who have hurt them to find release from guilt and an inner peace.

COMING TO TERMS WITH
OUR FAMILY OF ORIGIN

It took many years for me to realise how much we are shaped by our experience of the family in which we grew up, our family of origin. It is not being too dramatic to say that the experience we had in our first family is, to a very large degree, the thing that has made us the people we are as adults. Our values, attitudes and behaviours are all shaped by our family.

When we form a relationship with another person these influences affect the way we relate to one another. Of course, the values and attitudes we have differ from person to person, because all families are different. In Chapter Four, I talk about the different attitudes of families to death and dying. There are certain unspoken rules in families which govern the way they operate. For example, your family of origin may have had a rule that sex was never discussed openly, that there would never be any public display of affection or, in some cases, no public display of any emotion.

Often these rules are passed down through the generations and are never articulated and rarely challenged. If you are brave enough to challenge one of these unspoken conventions, you will quickly find that it will be defended with a great deal of energy. Behind the emotional outburst will be: 'This family has always operated like this. How dare you rock the boat? Are you saying that the way we've done it all these years is wrong?'

SHAPING ATTITUDES

In one family being thrifty, if not stingy, and avoiding the use of credit at all costs may have been encouraged. My father lived through the tough years of the Depression in Melbourne in the 1920s and 1930s. He remembers what it was like to have nothing but bread and dripping for dinner, sometimes even to go hungry. This shaped the attitudes of my parents' generation to money, possessions and credit. It was a maxim in our family that you never bought anything on credit. You waited until you had saved the money and then you bought it. If you didn't have the money in hand, it meant you couldn't afford to buy whatever it was you wanted.

The reaction of some people to this experience would be to feel that lavishing money on an expensive gift would be impossible. They would become misers, watching every cent, in those days every penny. But my father's reaction was to become generous with his money. He had gone without and he didn't want his children to have to do the same. So he has been a very generous father.

A CLASH OF ATTITUDES

Often a person who has grown up in a family that has handled money very carefully will be attracted to someone from a family in which costly gifts and dinners-out were a sign of the esteem in which a person was held. They are drawn to the generosity and apparent freedom of this attitude to giving. But what happens when there is a choice between buying expensive Christmas presents or paying off some of the mortgage? There is also potential for conflict between couples who were in different positions in their families of origin.

First children are used to getting their own way, something they learned while occupying that privileged position of an only child. If a first child marries a second child, there may be no problem, as the second child is used to doing what the oldest child wants.

However, if two first children get together, there will almost certainly be fireworks as a battle takes place to discover who is the strongest. Likewise in the area of communication. In the family of one partner, the word of the parents may have been law. If Dad said 'Jump!', the kids never dared ask why. Their instinctive response would be 'How high?' This was the way they showed love and respect for their parents. But the other partner may have come from a family in which the father encouraged discussion, often-lively debate around the dinner table at night. Margaret Andrews came from such folk. However, she quickly discovered that her new husband had come from a different kind of family:

At one stage, I recall voicing strongly my opinion on some subject about which I felt very emotional. My husband's response though was to challenge me to justify my stance. I was taken aback. 'Surely, if he loved me, he would take my word for it. He would accept my views and not argue the point with me.' Gradually, however, we realised that we were communicating in the different styles that we had learnt growing up. Neither was right or wrong, but these styles had a powerful impact on our relationship.[43]

One of the biggest conflicts in a relationship can occur over the way children are parented. Our family of origin is where we learn to parent.

Margaret Andrews writes:

Over the years we learnt more about each other's family backgrounds: how they did things, how they communicated, felt about money, handled conflict, brought up children and just had fun. As we learnt about our family backgrounds, we also learnt about ourselves and why we related to each other as we did. In my family, the dinner table was a warm babble of noise, with many conversations at once. In my husband's smaller family, only one person spoke at a time. I still recall feeling uncomfortable in the more reserved environment, which included occasional complete silence. This knowledge helped us better understand each other and allowed us to choose how we would do things as a new family.[44]

LEARNING NEW WAYS

It is only as we become aware of the ways we have been shaped by our family of origin that we can begin to change. It is only as we begin to understand why we react in the way we do that we can start to be freed to respond differently. My father's way of disciplining my sister and me as children was fairly authoritarian. He used the spoon and the strap, not often, but when he felt they were needed — if I got too out of line, which happened reasonably often if my memory serves me correctly. This is not a criticism of my father. The way my father disciplined his children was probably a result of the way he had been disciplined.

My parents' generation tended to discipline children in an authoritarian way. It is only in the past twenty years that new ways of handling children have been devised, as a result of techniques like Thomas Gordon's excellent Parent Effectiveness Training. These methods have provided parents with better ways of being families and disciplining children.

It is possible to break free from childhood influences and learn new ways of parenting. Margaret Andrews and her husband have succeeded in developing new methods of parenting:

> Our family table is a mixture of ... both our family backgrounds. By reflecting on our families of origin, we were able to reach a compromise that meant our family meal time was meaningful for us both.[45]

At a glance

Facing the past is the first step towards healing.

Forgiveness is the key to healing.

We can choose not to hate;
we can even choose to love.

CHAPTER FOUR

Facing the future

FACING THE INEVITABLE

What I am about to discuss may be difficult for some people to face because I want to focus on one of the least popular topics in human society — death. The ultimate reality of death and the fragility of life came home powerfully to us all in the tragic death of Princess Diana in Paris in 1997 in a car accident that should never have happened.

I have heard so many people describe how Diana's death had made them realise how short life can be.

However, some readers may not get past the first line of this chapter, as in my experience people in post-modern society, despite its sophistication and knowledge, fear death as much as ever. There seems to be so much of it. The truth of course is that there is no more death than there has ever been. Yet, when someone dies, especially someone as famous as the Princess of Wales or Mother Teresa, we hear about it within moments.

A hundred years ago the news filtered around the world slowly and people had time to come to terms with terrible tragedy in a gentler way. But now the media brings us every gory detail almost as it happens. There is no chance to absorb the details slowly. We see it all in graphic colour before our eyes and it can simply traumatise us. It can be too much to take in. And then we have the endless media analysis of what took place, which often traumatises people further. Some people I have met seem to spend a great deal of energy avoiding ever encountering even the faintest glimmer of the thought of death, but if there is an absolute inevitability in life it is that we shall all die one day. Most people I know don't think about dying very much.

FEARING DEATH TAKES ENERGY
FROM THE PRESENT

Worrying about dying can consume a great deal of our emotional energy in the present if we haven't faced its inevitability. I'm not suggesting we should become preoccupied with the thought of dying, as some people do. But unless we have faced its inevitability, it can hamper our ability to live fully in the moment.

It's been said that dying is a truly universal human custom. We all do it sooner or later! Most of us are scared of the thought of death or of the process of dying. I'm not scared of death because as a follower of Christ I know where I'm going and with whom I'm going to spend eternity. But I'm less enthusiastic about the process of dying. I have no desire to die a slow lingering death or to die violently, although I know that ultimately this is something over which I will have no control. But, no matter how much we dislike thinking about it, sooner or later each of us is going to die. Death is part of life. From the moment we're born we begin to die. There is, though, another reason that most of us struggle with death, and that is that death in our society is remote.

THE SANITISATION OF DEATH

The only dead bodies most of us will ever see are on the TV screen, at the cinema or in the newspaper. Death and dying don't really touch us. Death has been sanitised in Western society. In two-thirds of the world, it is a daily, concrete, blood and guts affair. But, not in the West. Death and dying have been hidden away in hospitals, old people's homes and funeral parlours. When we have a loved one die chances are they will die in hospital or an old people's home. If they do happen to die at home we have trained professionals, undertakers, who will come and take them away and prepare them for burial.

The funeral directors I deal with are wonderful people who do their jobs very professionally and caringly. Dealing with death is probably one of the first jobs that families began to 'outsource' to trained professionals and I can in one sense understand why. However, I wonder if hiring professionals to deal with death is the most healthy way for us to face it as a society. Even a hundred years ago when a family member died, they would be laid out in the front room of the house, where they could be visited until the funeral. That was what the front room was designed for.

Loving friends or relatives would wash and dress the body and prepare the dead person for burial. This process helped people enormously in their grieving. It enabled them to accept far more quickly the death of their loved one and helped them to say goodbye. It also took away the fear of death. A fear of dead bodies results from a fear of disease, but very few people in our society die of infectious diseases.

TOUCHING IS HEALTHY

We are not going to catch cancer or coronary heart disease by touching a dead body. It can be helpful to touch the body of a loved one who has died — to hold them and to kiss them goodbye. I had never seen anyone die, or even a dead body, until the first year of my curacy as a minister. One day I was called to the hospital to pray for a parishioner who was dying. I sat by his bedside and prayed for him and his family. While I was there, he died. The experience was quite awesome. One moment he was a gravely ill person, the next he was dead. His life force, his spirit, left him, and what was left was just the empty shell of someone who had once been human.

It was an experience I will never forget, because watching someone die is in many ways like watching someone be born. It is something that is totally beyond our control. The person who is dying is completely helpless. There is nothing they can do to stop themselves from dying and there is nothing we can do to stop it either.

I don't want to sound too romantic about death, because it can be both stark and terrifying. But there is a mystery about a person dying, the depths of which we can never plumb. And being fully involved in the process of a loved one dying can only be a good and healthy thing.

We need to bring death out into the open and talk about it, instead of pushing it under the carpet. We tend to want to cover up the truth as if somehow it will protect us and our loved ones. I have observed many families who decide not to tell the truth to a loved one who has been diagnosed with a terminal disease: 'We won't tell them how sick they are because, if we do, they might drop their bundle emotionally,' is the reason given for covering up the truth. But don't people who have potentially terminal diseases have the right to know the truth? What right do we have to hide the truth from them?

Often people are very angry when they later discover they were not told they had a fatal disease, because they felt they had been denied the opportunity of beginning to prepare for dying. Very often, too, the reason people are not told the truth is far from altruistic. It's because we feel we wouldn't cope with them being told. It would force us to face the pain of the reality of the diagnosis. This is all part of our attempts in our death-denying society to hide death away. However, there are some signs of a more healthy attitude to death in our society.

One such sign is the recent publication of *The Penguin Book of Death*, a series of essays that tackle the issues of death and dying in a very frank, no-holds barred way.[46] The more we can do to encourage open discussion of death and dying in our community the more emotionally healthy we will be and the more effectively we will live in the moment. We need to be discussing death and dying from the earliest age, both in our homes and in appropriate ways in school curricula. And if we resist the idea of addressing these issues in primary school because we feel 'it's all a bit too morbid' we need to ask ourselves: is it our fear of death that feeds our reservations? Surely the more honest we are about death the more healthily we can live.

ENRICHING THE PRESENT
BY FACING THE FUTURE

Our fear of dying can rob us of life here and now. The bottom line for all of us is that in a hundred years' time we will not be alive. I have an electronic organiser which provides a calendar up to the year 2099 and it was a strange feeling recently to look at the year 2070 and to think, 'I'm not going to be alive then because I'm not going to live to be 120!' Facing our mortality can only be a good thing because it releases us to live more fully in the present moment instead of draining our energies by trying to suppress our fears of dying.

In his book *Further Along the Road Less Travelled*, M. Scott Peck writes that, 'The knowledge that life is limited fills many of us with a sense of meaninglessness. Since we're going to be chopped down by the Grim Reaper like so much straw, what possible meaning could there be to our paltry human existence?'[47]

However, he goes on to say that rather than stripping our lives of meaning death can give them more meaning. He suggests that:

Death is a magnificent lover. If you are suffering from a sense of meaningless or ennui, there is nothing better I can suggest to you than to strike up a serious relationship with the end of your existence. Like any great love, death is full of mystery and that's where much of the excitement comes from. Because as you struggle with the mystery of your death, you will discover the meaning of your life.[48]

Peck also quotes the humanitarian Albert Schweitzer, who wrote:

We must all become familiar with the thought of death if we want to become really good people. We need not think of it every day or every hour. But when the path of life leads us to some vantage point where the scene around us fades away and we contemplate the distant view right to the end, let us not close our eyes. Let us pause for that moment, look at the distant view and then carry on. Thinking about death in this way produces love for life. When we are familiar with death we accept each week, each day, as a gift. Only if we are able to accept life — bit by bit — does it become precious.[49]

However, accepting our own mortality is something that doesn't happen easily or quickly. I vividly remember the first suicide I dealt with in parish ministry. The man had hanged himself and for nights afterwards I would wake from dreaming with a mind full of pictures and words spoken by family members. I even imagined myself hanging from a noose. On reflection, I came to see that rather than some kind of Freudian death-wish, I was again struggling with my own mortality. There would one day be a metaphorical noose of death around my neck. My body would one day also be put in a wooden box for friends and relatives to come and view. I was not going to live forever.

It has been said of pastoral carers that the extent to which they are able to accept their own mortality will determine the extent to which they are able to help those who are bereaved. I believe this principle also holds true for living in the moment. The extent to which we accept the inevitability of our own death will affect our ability to live in the moment.

IN THE FACE OF DEATH

The writer on spirituality Henri Nouwen is someone who faced death after being hit by a car. He was walking along an icy road near his home in Canada one mid-winter's morning when he was hit in the back by the side mirror of a passing car. At first, it didn't feel as though much damage had been done, but when he was taken to hospital doctors discovered he had five broken ribs. Then he began to feel very ill, became dizzy and felt like vomiting. Henri was bleeding internally. Ultra-sound testing revealed the bleeding was coming from his spleen, and his condition grew steadily worse. Doctors performed an emergency operation to remove the spleen in an attempt to save his life. Henri Nouwen writes:

> What I experienced then was something I had never experienced before: pure and unconditional love. Better still, what I experienced was an intensely personal presence that pushed all my fears aside and said, 'Come. Don't be afraid. I love you.' A very gentle, non-judgemental presence, a presence that simply asked me to trust completely. I hesitate to speak simply about Jesus, because of my concern that the name of Jesus might not evoke the full divine presence that I experienced. It was not a warm light, a rainbow or an open door that I saw, but a human yet divine presence that I felt, inviting me to come closer and to let go of all my fears.[50]

Nouwen says that facing death and putting his life totally into the hands of Jesus, whom he had spent his whole life following and seeking to serve, was for him a transforming experience:

> My whole life had been an arduous attempt to follow Jesus as I had come to know him through my parents, friends and teachers. I had spent countless hours studying the Bible, listening to lectures and sermons, and reading spiritual books. Jesus has been very close to me, but also very distant, a friend, but also a stranger, a source of hope, but also of fear, guilt and shame. But now, when I walked around the portal of death, all ambiguity and all uncertainty were gone.
>
> He was there, the Lord of my life, saying, 'Come to me, come.'[51]

Henri Nouwen said that the overwhelming emotion was that of homecoming.

COMING TO TERMS WITH
OUR OWN MORTALITY

Tony De Mello suggests the exercise of imagining seeing our own body laid in a coffin following our death. Some people may feel this is an unhealthy thing to do, but in my experience facing reality is never unhealthy. De Mello suggests finding time and a quiet place to do this exercise:

Imagine you see your body in the coffin laid out for the funeral rites. ... Take a good look at your body, especially at the expression on your face ...

Now look at all the people who have come to your funeral ... Go slowly from one pew to another looking into their faces ... Stop before each person and guess what they are thinking and feeling ...

Now listen to the eulogy. Who is the speaker? How do you feel about what is being said? Can you accept all the good things being said about you? ... If you cannot, study your resistance to accepting it ...

Look again at the faces of the friends who have come to your funeral ... Imagine the good things they will be saying about you when the funeral is over ... Is there something you would like to say to each of them before they leave, some final farewell in response to all they are thinking and feeling about you, a response which, alas, they will never hear now?... say it, all the same, and see what it does to you ...

The funeral rites are over. You now stand above the grave in which your body lies, watching your friends leave the cemetery. What are your feelings as you stand there and look back on your life and your experiences ... Was it all worthwhile? ...

Now become aware of your existence in the room and realise you are still alive and still have time at your disposal ... Do you see your friends differently as a result of this exercise? Do you feel differently about yourself? ...[52]

MAKING THE MOST OF THE TIME WE HAVE

One of the people who influenced me most in my teenage years was a man called Doug. He was one of the most caring, wise and compassionate people I have ever known. He had a unique strength, gentleness and attractiveness.

He was simply a wonderful human being. In fact, he and his wife, Grace, had a great influence on my life.

I remember with much gratitude their love and mentoring of me in my teenage years. Doug was diagnosed with bowel cancer and died from it in 1994. He told me that he was part of a cancer support group at a Sydney hospital. Just a few weeks before he died, he rang me one night from Sydney. He told me that the previous year had been the richest of his life, because he had faced head-on the reality that he may not be on Earth for much longer. He had been very open in talking to his family about his condition and they had been very honest with him. He said that a number of the people in his cancer support group were homosexual men who were HIV positive. Doug said it had been a humbling experience to be part of the group and to have the opportunity to share the Christian hope he had for the future with these men, who in many cases had given up hope.

Another friend, Jim, has had cancer for a number of years. To help him face up to his own mortality, he decided to make his own coffin. He did so, not only because it is cheaper than buying one but also because it is therapeutic.

He uses the coffin as a coffee table in his lounge room. He told me that the act of making the box his dead body would one day lie in helped him to begin to come to terms with the inevitability of his own death. Some people he knows think that building his own coffin was a strange, if not perverse, thing to have done. How morbid can you get? On the contrary, I think it is a very healthy thing he has done, which will do a great deal to help him and his family face reality.

LIVING A DAY AT A TIME

Not only do we fear future events that are certain to happen, like death, but we also often fear things that will not take place. I am someone who has struggled with anxiety for most of my life. My anxiety tends to focus on my health, so I have grappled with all sorts of fears about my health over the years, all of which have been totally groundless so far.

Dale Carnegie writes of a young soldier during the Second World War. Towards the end of the war the soldier was brought in to the army dispensary suffering from what we now call post-traumatic stress syndrome. The soldier's job was to help set up and maintain records of all men killed in action, missing in action and hospitalised. He had to gather up the personal effects of those who had died and send them back to their families. He also had to help bury the bodies of both Allied and German war dead, which was a very stressful job. He became so stressed that he lost fifteen kilos and was on the verge of a complete breakdown. The army doctor told the young man he would not survive unless he learned to control his anxiety and carry out his job one thing at a time, like each grain of sand going through the neck of an hourglass.[53]

Carnegie says he has practised this philosophy ever since, 'One grain of sand at a time ... one task at a time.' Our main business is not to see what lies dimly at a distance but to do what lies clearly at hand. We need to live in what he calls 'day-tight compartments'. Certainly, we think about and plan for the future, but we choose to focus our energies on living this day, this present moment.[54]

LIVE THIS DAY AS YOUR LAST DAY

Another way of living more fully in the moment is to say to yourself at the beginning of a day, 'I'm going to live this day as if it were my last.' I once heard a man with full-blown AIDS say, 'The only difference between me and other people is that I know my life is going to be shorter than I expected it to be.'

I find that if I have in the back of my mind the thought that this could be my last day on Earth it enables me to make more of each moment in that day. Obviously whether you can comfortably do this depends on the extent to which you have come to terms with the inevitability of your own death. I have no doubts about what will happen when I die, so I find this quite a liberating way to begin a day. Mind you, I don't do it every day. But, from time to time I live a day like this and it's a very helpful thing to do.

THE FUTURE — A DANGEROUS PLACE TO TRY TO SEE

We live in a world which, to a very large extent, lives in the future. For many people today the present is a difficult and unhappy place, so they focus on the future. We plan for the future. We set aside money for the future. We gamble in the hope of winning a financially secure future, in the mistaken belief that money can buy happiness. We worry about the future.

Over the past decade fear and anxiety about the future have resulted in a surge of interest in trying to discover what the future will bring. Men and women have, from antiquity, tried to foretell the future, but in recent years fortune-telling has almost become a de facto religion in Australia. It is impossible to open a magazine or newspaper that doesn't contain an astrological column attempting to predict our futures in the stars. There are even 0055 numbers that enable people to ring psychics and fortune-tellers who claim to be able to predict the future.

Reading the stars has become almost another form of identifying personality types and is regarded by most people as a harmless, if not fun, thing to do. However, I believe we are not designed to live in the future or to know what the future will bring. We are designed to live in the present.

As Margaret Houston has said, slightly tongue in cheek, 'If I could see the future, I would be appalled. I am sure I wouldn't approve of it at all. I will live it when it comes to me. I know it will be meaningful because it will be the result of this meaningful present moment.'

The Christian scriptures suggest it is very unwise to try to predict the future. The Old Testament book of Deuteronomy warns against practising black magic or witchcraft to tell fortunes or to cast spells or to talk to spirits of the dead (Chapter 18, verse 10ff). I understand why people have a fascination with the future, but in the end I believe it's a question of where we put our trust. Do we trust our future to God or to the astrologers? I know where I choose to put my trust. Leaving aside the Bible's warnings, how much sense does it make to try to discover what the future will bring? The motivation to discover the future is anxiety over what it will bring, but what if a fortune-teller predicts I will die in a car accident or of cancer or that my loved ones will die a terrible death? If their prediction is accurate will it make me less or more fearful about the future? Knowing what the future will bring doesn't guarantee that the future can be changed. In fact, believing something terrible will happen in the future will make me far more anxious, and if the prediction is false — but I believe it to be true — it may well become a self-fulfilling prophecy.

If a person believes strongly enough that they are going to die in a certain way, it is likely that they will die in that way. This is not superstition or magic, but the power of the human mind. The Aboriginal custom of pointing the bone proves the point. When an Aboriginal, or indeed anyone else, believes they will die if the death bone is pointed at them, they will. There is a great deal of sense in not trying to discover what the future will bring. As Jesus said, each day has enough troubles of its own. We are given the strength to cope with one day at a time. We don't need the anxiety caused by having our futures foretold.

FALSE EXPECTATIONS ABOUT THE FUTURE

In childhood, we can have created within us a huge range of expectations that are often totally unrealistic. One of those expectations is what I call the myth of eternal romance. For me children's stories, the media and family expectations conspired to create within me a belief that one day I would meet the perfect woman. Her eyes would catch mine the first time we met and we would be in love. She would have a sensational figure, be a sparkling conversationalist no matter how tired she felt, would be an incredible cook and would always want sex.

It didn't quite happen like that. I am married to a very attractive woman and I love her very much. But she isn't always a sparkling conversationalist, especially when she's tired. And she doesn't always feel like sex. Nor do I. Life just isn't like that, no matter what the myths about sexuality are as propagated by *Dolly* and *Elle* magazines. The reality of permanent relationships is that it's hard work to stay with the same person. Romance and physical attraction are not a firm enough foundation for a lasting relationship. The story of the love of Rose and Jack in the film *Titanic* is a wonderful story, but it's very much a reflection of the twentieth century mythology of romance. Love is much more about lifelong commitment than it is about butterflies in the stomach or feeling turned on. Romance is part of a love relationship, but it's not the foundation. A decision to remain committed to each other no matter what life may bring is a foundation that will last. In the end love is a choice. It is possible to fall in love and then out of it. Romance may fade, but if we choose to continue to love the romance will return.

M. Scott Peck begins his best-selling book *The Road Less Travelled* with the hardly startling observation that life is difficult.[55] While this may seem obvious because of the number of problems most of us face daily, many people seem to struggle to accept that life is difficult. They operate on the belief that life should be straightforward, virtually problem-free. I've noticed that many religious people seem to operate on this basis. I did for almost half my life. The thinking goes something like this: 'Because God is in control of my life all will go smoothly. I won't have many problems, at least not any major ones.' But experience teaches us that life isn't like that. We face a huge range of problems every day of our lives. God promises to be with us in the problems and to give us the strength to cope, not to provide us with a problem-free life.

However, if we operate on false expectations about the future, we can find the weight of these problems crushing. I can think of people I've met who forever bemoan their hassles and problems. They feel life isn't fair. Somehow they ended up with the short straw. Things always go wrong for them. It took me many years to realise that problems are normal. It took a few more years to realise that I could choose how to respond to the problems life brings. Does that sound naive? Well maybe it was but I suspect I'm not alone. What brought me to this realisation was the experience of a friend of mine whose brother got ME (myalgic encephalomyelitis or chronic fatigue syndrome). My friend was told by his brother, 'I got chronic fatigue syndrome because mum and dad divorced.' However, my friend, who had realised he was able to choose how he would react to life's problems, said, 'No, you didn't get ME because mum and dad split up. You got it because of your response to their divorce.'

This is one of the deepest principles of life. What determines how well we cope with our problems is how we react to them. This seems blindingly obvious to anyone who understands this truth, but it is not obvious to those who don't. I lived half my life without realising it. I came to see that there is absolutely nothing we can do to prevent problems occurring in our lives. However, there is everything we can do about the way we react to those problems.

At a glance

Accepting our own mortality frees us to
live more fully in the moment.

Don't try to see into the future; live life today,
a day at a time.

Problems are a normal part of life —
it is our choice how we deal with them.

CHAPTER FIVE

Tuning in to the present

OUR CULTURE OF BUSYNESS

If we are to develop a higher quality of life, the first step is to recognise that there are many ways to deal with issues rather than one single one. I ask people to consider a change in the success criteria they feel important. I want them to move from valuing the quantity of goods to the quality of life, from being overwhelmed by information to valuing knowledge and wisdom.

Even when we do take time off from work, we find it hard to make best use of it. We work hard at leisure. My personality type in the Myer–Briggs scheme is an ENTJ.

I am a natural leader and love organising others and making plans for the future. But when it comes to leisure I can struggle. I find it hard just to relax and recreate as an end in itself. I feel guilty just playing. Writing in *Sojourners* magazine, American commentator on spirituality Jim Rice traces the origins of our inability to fully enjoy our leisure back to the Industrial Age:

> Bankers and manufacturers felt that the best way to get an honest day's work was to encourage thriftiness, seriousness, and abstention and discourage 'idleness.' Adam Smith, in *The Wealth of Nations*, argued that activity is only truly productive if it takes raw material and makes it into something useful; the idle produce nothing. The Renaissance doctrine that it is through work alone that a human produces and knows became the guiding principle of the 19th century — a philosophy embraced not only by followers of free-marketeer Smith, but by socialists, communists, 'scientific' thinkers, and utopians as well. Idleness as the devil's playground was a long way from the ideal of leisure as essential to civilisation.
>
> As the 19th century wound down, a new phenomenon emerged. More and more workers had money in their

pockets beyond that needed for the essentials of life, and — no surprise here — entrepreneurs rushed to fill the need for something to do with that extra money. Between 1850 and 1900, businesses grew that profited from after-work spending. Amusements that had been recently condemned as 'frivolous' took on new meaning — and acceptance — as they began to be seen as potential revenue sources.

Rice writes that:

Even what people did for fun changed from free games such as quoits, bowls, and rabbit-coursing to pay-per-view entertainment such as boxing, golf and football. Not coincidentally, the very language used to describe these after-hours carousings was transformed as well. The word 'idleness' faded from usage, and the word 'leisure' began to emerge. What was being born, of course, has now become the multi-billion-dollar industry of play. Our culture provides a steady drumbeat of advertising that not only sells us the myriad things we must have to fill our free time, but offers wondrous time savers to create more of it. Now we are not only encouraged to work hard, but we are instructed that we have to play hard as well.[56]

SLOW DOWN, YOU'RE GOING TOO FAST

Tasmania, where I live, is one of the most beautiful places in the world. There is a diversity of landscape here and a rugged wilderness that has attracted people from all over the world. But it is only when we open our eyes and take time to see what is around us by living the moment that we will appreciate the beauty and subtlety of our world. Simon and Garfunkel encouraged us back in the slow-moving 1960s to slow down because we were moving too fast, but we didn't take their advice. Life has become faster and faster and more and more complex. We seem to have less and less time, despite all the inventions designed to save time. We have no safety margin left. We're pushed to the limit with nothing left in reserve. So when we get to the top of a flight of stairs, there's no air left in our lungs. When we get to the end of a busy week there's no energy left in our bodies. So often we are running on empty, and that's the beginning of burnout.

We can live impoverished lives because we don't slow down. We're going too fast. Even when we do slow down, our minds may be elsewhere and we can be distracted and tired and weighed down with the burdens of the day. There is only one way to combat this kind of distractedness, once we become aware of it. We have to make a conscious effort to tune in to the present, to focus all our attention on what we are doing and to be there for whoever we are with in that moment.

There is in the Old Testament book of Psalms a very peculiar little Hebrew word which none of the biblical scholars has ever succeeded in accurately translating. It is the word *selah*, which appears to mean 'stop/pause'. I think it's a timely word for our world as we head into a new millennium. Stop and pause. Slow down. Look around. Take time to smell the roses and to look into each other's faces. Take time to reflect on life. Where am I headed? What am I doing? Is what I'm doing contributing to this world I'm part of?

ARE YOU DRIVEN?

It may be helpful to ask yourself the question: 'Am I driven and if so by what?' People who are driven are very often motivated by guilt and fear. There is so much that can drive us in today's world — a desire for money, power, fame, status, comfort, possessions. The demands of a job may cause a person to spend a great deal of time, effort and energy doing things that ultimately are of little real value. Following the death of my son James I came to see that only one thing in life matters. All that matters in life are my relationships — with God, my family and friends. I can lose everything else in life, but if I still have relationships with those I love I can keep going. Fostering those relationships in the present should be a very high priority in our lives.

DEVELOPING GREATER AWARENESS

I have come to realise that we don't need a huge repertoire of techniques to live life more fully. Sometimes, all we need do is become more aware of each moment as we live it. I am the kind of person who can be oblivious to my environment. Some women feel this is a common male trait! I am capable of failing to notice the colour of a dress or other details. I have noticed over the years that many males exhibit a disturbing degree of distraction. I have to work hard at being aware of my environment. I can drive the same road again and again without really noticing the colour of the hills and the geography as I sail past. This can be the result of preoccupation with the busyness of life, but in my case is just my personality type. I simply tend not to see the detail of things and as a result I have to make a conscious, focused effort to enjoy the beauty of the world around me.

One of our problems as post-modern people is that we tend to live too much in our heads. We are not nearly conscious enough of our senses. I became aware of my tendency to live in my head when my father was dying of cancer two years ago. I came to see that intellectualising my emotions was a way of keeping control over my feelings. I was afraid that if I really let myself feel I might be embarrassed or vulnerable. This was my Dad who was dying not someone else's father. I wanted to let those feelings out but at the same time I was afraid to. So I pushed my feelings into my head by analysing what I was experiencing instead of allowing myself to feel. I could very eloquently describe the emotions, but I wasn't feeling them, which meant that a whole part of me was being held in tight check. Not a healthy state. Writer on spirituality Anthony De Mello suggests this helpful exercise:

live the moment

Close your eyes. I am now going to ask you to become aware of some sensations in your body that you are feeling at this moment but are not explicitly aware of.

Become aware of the touch of your clothes on your shoulders ... or of your back touching the chair you're sitting on ...

Now be aware of the feel of your hands as they touch each other or rest on your lap ...

Now become conscious of your thighs or your buttocks pressing against the chair ...

Now focus on the feel of the soles of your feet as they touch your shoes ...

Once again: your shoulders ... your back ... your right hand ... your left hand ... your thighs ... your feet ...

Again: shoulders ... back ... right hand ... left hand ... right thigh ... left thigh ... right foot ...

Continue to go round moving from one part of your body to another. Don't dwell for more than a few seconds on each part, shoulders, back, and thighs as you move from one part to another ...

Dwell on the parts of your body I've suggested or on any other part you wish: your head, neck, arms, chest, stomach … The important thing is that you get the feel, the sensation of each part; that you feel it for a second or two, and then move on to another part of the body …

After five minutes open your eyes and end the exercise.[57]

The purpose of this exercise is to get us more in touch with the experience of our senses. However, it is not always as simple as it sounds. De Mello points out that some people when asked to feel their arms and legs and hands don't really feel them, but instead produce a mental picture of these limbs — their size, their shape, their location in the body. It took me many years to realise I was doing this. I am often not in touch with my senses. To get more in touch with our senses, Tony De Mello suggests:

Feel the heat or cold of the atmosphere around you. Feel the breeze as it caresses your body. Feel the heat of the sun making contact with your skin. Feel the texture and temperature of the object you are touching…and see what a difference it makes. See how you come alive by coming to the present. Once you have mastered this technique of sense awareness you will be surprised to see what it can do for you if you are the type that worries about the future or feels guilty about the past.

However, De Mello says we may, at first, feel sensations in only a small part of the surface of these limbs, or perhaps not at all. Living in our heads for years and years may have deadened our sensibility. So we may need to persist with these exercises for some time before we notice any effect:

> Close your eyes again and get in touch with sensations in various parts of your body . . .
>
> The ideal would be not to think of the various parts of your body as 'hands' or 'legs' or 'back', but just to move from one sensation to another and give no labels or names either to your limbs or to the sensations you experience in them.
>
> If you feel the urge to move or to change position don't give in to it. Just become aware of the urge; don't give in to it. Just become aware of the urge and the bodily discomfort.[58]

THE BEAUTY OF THE WORLD WE LIVE IN

We live in an extraordinarily beautiful world. Yet often we are so busy, and so anxious, that we fail to see what is all around us. Cellist Pablo Casals addresses this issue in his autobiography:

> For the past eighty years I have started each day in the same manner. It is not a mechanical routine but something essential to my daily life. I go to the piano and I play two preludes and fugues of Bach. I cannot think of doing otherwise. It is a sort of benediction on the house. But, that is not the only meaning it has for me. It is a rediscovery of the world of which I have the joy of being a part. It fills me with the awareness of the wonder of life, with a feeling of the incredible marvel of being a human being — do not think that a day has passed in my life in which I have failed to look with fresh amazement at the miracle of nature. The world around us is miraculous, despite the damage the human race has inflicted on it.[59]

Long-time friend and environmentalist Peter Grant writes beautifully about the world around us and our place in it:

> I am sitting, day-dreaming. Perhaps I should be studying, or writing, or at least thinking. But what passes through my mind has no more consistency than a winter mist. Then a butcher bird lands on the tree outside my window.

In its bill is a writhing black lizard. Without warning, the bird flies straight at me, crashing beak-first, or in this case lizard-first — into the glass of the window. It loops around, returns and repeats the action thrice more, until the lizard hangs limp and digestible. The butcher bird then flies off to finish its meal. I am fully awake now. My eyes have seen, my ears have heard, and my imagination is filling in the rest of the drama. Will the bird tear its prey apart, as its name implies, before eating it? Or will it swallow the hapless reptile in one gulp? Life and death and the present moment have suddenly snapped into focus out of the midst of my mind.

Peter Grant says:

I have been told this world is not my home. I am spirit; I am just passing through; heaven is my home. You may have heard it too. I no longer believe it. At least I no longer believe in that casual separation of spirit and matter, as though God is only interested in ghosts. We are not given bodies for nothing. God didn't create a cosmos full of matter, and then declare it 'good — very good' for no reason. Neither did God take human form as Jesus Christ to save only 'souls'.

The butcher bird's sudden appearance at my window has reminded me of some of these realities. It has also reminded me, in a small but startling way, of the reality of life and death. I recall that Job was told:

> *But ask the beasts and they will teach you;*
> *the birds of the air and they will tell you;*
> *or the plants of the earth and they will teach you;*
> *and the fish of the sea will declare to you.*
> *Who among all these does not know*
> *That the hand of the Lord has done this?*
> *In his hand is the life of every living thing*
> *And the breath of all humankind.*
>
> *(Job Chapter 12: verses 7–10 N.I.V.)*

Jesus, a great observer of the natural world, came from the same tradition. He pointed towards plants and animals; seasons and signs. He once remarked that 'not a sparrow falls to the earth without my Father knowing'. I suspect the same goes for lizards.[60]

WHAT'S REALLY IMPORTANT?

One of the greatest lessons I have learned is that my worth as a human being is not measured by what I do but by who I am. The Bible story of Mary and Martha drives home the need to get our being right before our doing. Jesus drops in to visit his friends Martha and Mary. He finds Martha too busy to stop while Mary makes time to sit and talk. Clive Sansom's poem 'Martha of Bethany' helps highlight the issues:

> *It's all very well*
> *Sitting in the shade of the courtyard*
> *Talking about your souls.*
> *Someone's got to see to the cooking,*
> *Standing at the oven all morning*
> *With the two of you taking your ease.*
> *It's all very well saying he'd be content*
> *With bread and honey.*
> *Perhaps he would — but I wouldn't,*
> *Coming to our house like this,*
> *Not giving him of our best.*
> *Yes it's all very well*
> *Him trying to excuse you,*

Saying your recipe's best,
Saying I worry too much,
That I'm always anxious.
Someone's got to worry —
And double if the others don't care.
For it's all very well
Talking of faith and belief
But what would you do
If everyone sat in the cool
Not getting their meals?
And he can't go wandering
On an empty stomach —
He'd die in the first fortnight.
Then where would you be
With all your discussions and questions
And no one to answer them?
It's all very well. [61]

'Being' and 'doing' are both essential in life as Martha so succinctly points out. If we don't spend time 'doing' meals we die. However, as Martha discovered in this story we can miss out on important things in life if we're busy doing when we should be 'being'. Jesus criticised Martha, not because she was preparing a meal for them, but because she was preparing such an elaborate meal when he had important things to tell her as well as Mary. He was saying, 'Look, Martha, a sandwich will do. Come and listen because I have important things to tell you.'

'BE' BEFORE YOU 'DO'

We live in a world that majors on doing. Ambition and achievement are among the idols of our generation. The first question a person is asked socially is, 'What do you do?' Fortunately people are beginning to become a little more sensitive to the realities of unemployment and not asking this question so indiscriminately. I tend to ask people how they occupy their time rather than what they do. Nevertheless what you do seems to define your status in the world. If you are unemployed or someone who spends their time caring for children you are likely to be regarded less highly than a person with a paid job, whether full or part time. Old people and mothers who look after children full time instead of going out to paid work are seen as being of little value to society. The danger of defining our place in the world by what we do or don't do is that this criterion may also decide our worth as human beings in our own eyes and in the eyes of others. I believe many people struggle with being and doing.

CHILDREN CAN BE OUR TEACHERS

Children possess the ability to live in the present far better than we do as adults. My children have been my teachers. My youngest daughters, Catherine, who is six, and Elizabeth, who is nine, mentor me in living in the moment. Today Catherine and I went for a walk around our neighbourhood. My idea of a walk is to get from one place to another as swiftly as possible and as energetically as possible, to make it beneficial in terms of exercise. A pragmatic way of walking. Not so Catherine. She walks more slowly than I do, not only because her legs are shorter than mine, but also because she's far more interested in the scenery. We stopped to follow 'the trail of a snail' on the footpath — really cracks in the pavement, but not to her. The snail 'went up a driveway and disappeared into a hole'. She picked flowers on the way 'to bring home for Mummy'. We also stopped to pick up a 'J' on the footpath, a stick in the shape of the letter 'J', which she then used as a 'longer arm' to touch flowers and plants that caught her attention. Catherine stopped briefly to use her 'J' to do battle with 'a monster' which threatened to attack us. She then stopped to pick more flowers along the way. It made me slow down too. For the first time in a long time I felt the warmth of the sun on my skin and the breeze on my face.

LEARNING TO LIVE IN A CHILDLIKE WAY

Children are very much focused in the present. Even as I write Catherine sits at my elbow, having just had my record of our walk read to her: 'I want it finished today' — my book she means. Regaining our imagination is another gift children can give us. They haven't lost their imagination yet or had it pummelled out of them at school. My daughter Elizabeth is a master at living in the moment. She loves imaginary games, which she and Catherine play for hours on end. The games enable them to enter fully into the experience of the moment. The game is all there is.

Elizabeth also loves to sit on my lap and wrap her arms around my neck and hug. When Elizabeth hugs she closes her eyes and snuggles in tight. She is an expert hugger. She does it with her whole being. The past and the future disappear from view. Only the hug matters. It is a wonderful feeling. This is something we need to relearn in adulthood.

Jesus once said that unless we change and become like children, we will never enter the kingdom of heaven (Matthew 18, verse 4). He may have been thinking of the humility, purity, innocence and honesty of a young child. However, the most obvious thing about a young child is its helplessness. Little children depend on their parents for their every need.

Could it not be that Jesus is saying that to enter God's kingdom we need to be like dependent, trusting, little children? While we can't go back to that 'blissful, uncomplicated existence' we can learn from children by choosing to build into our lives some of their characteristics. Life is not simple, but we can choose to make it simpler by choosing to live the moment before us in the way young children do.

SEVEN STEPS TO BETTER LEISURE

Jim Rice suggests that 'the commercialisation of leisure is in many ways the exact opposite of God's original plan for the human race.'[62] He lists seven ways in which we can begin to think differently about leisure:

1 It's OK to play. Most of us grew up with stories like The Little Red Hen (moral: you don't work, you don't eat) and The Tortoise and the Hare (you linger, you lose), tales that illustrated for us the consequences of too much play. Those who didn't keep their noses to the proverbial grindstone usually suffered for their idleness. (He argues that we need not only affirm the value of play, but also recognise its necessity and accept it as a gift from God.)

2 Leisure should be seen as an end in itself. Our culture is driven by results, and let's face it, so are many of us. Even our play is often motivated by a desire to produce something or accomplish something — even if it's only a lower heart rate or cholesterol count. (We ought to cherish leisure for its own sake, celebrate joyfulness

simply because it's a good thing, and accept that music or art or contemplation or play is intrinsically good and doesn't need any other justification.)

3   The commodification of leisure is a spiritual matter, and needs to be acknowledged as such and resisted. While advertising implies an equation between what we pay and how much fun we have, there's actually no necessary connection between money spent and enjoyment. (Yes, para-sailing at forty dollars an hour or snow skiing can be fun and exciting. But, so can a free game of volleyball at a picnic or a game of Monopoly with your children.)

4   Individual self-fulfilment is not enough. God's intention for creation is summarised in the biblical concept of shalom, which entails the pursuit of wholeness, of fullness of being, including beauty, goodness, truth, and joy. Shalom involves by definition a social dimension. (No individual fulfilment is possible apart from the building of relationships and seeking the welfare of the whole community. In other words, bowling alone just won't cut it.)

5   Leisure is not about what we watch but what we do.
    A key aspect of the commercialisation of leisure has
    been the growth of spectator sports. Sedentary activities
    in general are among the most regular ones for most of
    us: TV, reading, driving, meetings, lectures, visiting,
    dining out, theatre and concerts, playing cards. (But it's
    important to note that sedentariness is not the same as
    passivity or indolence. 'Active' and 'passive' are over-
    simplified categories, especially because it is hard to
    measure activity of the mind.)

6   The quality of leisure is directly related to broader
    questions about simplicity of life. (Many people
    couldn't 'afford' to work shorter hours and take less
    pay, even if given the option, because to do so would
    mean being unable to buy the things that advertising
    dangles in front of our eyes. Freeing ourselves from
    reliance on material things opens many life-enhancing
    possibilities.)

7   The amenities of modern life don't necessarily enhance
    our experience of leisure. A community of Amish people

was once offered a television set. Their response: 'If we were to add television to our lives, what would we take away? Conversation with our children? Reading? Praying?' They graciously declined. (We don't often stop to consider what we 'take away' when we make such additions to our lives.)[63]

Rice suggests that as we seek to approach leisure in a more intentional, spiritually grounded way, we don't do so in a vacuum. Our culture of busyness, the pace of our lives, directly affects the quality of our leisure. We should be careful not to romanticise the past. People (especially on the lower end of the income scale) have always had to work hard to scrape out a living. But a century ago, and in some cultures still today, the slower tempo of daily life meant less tension and more time for themselves and for each other. In the contemporary work world, many of us leave home for much of the day, hurriedly battle rush-hour traffic, arrive home tired and spent, eat our evening meal, and then face a long list of household chores. Western society, far from encouraging spiritual leisure or even the pursuit of happiness, inflicts as a norm the disease of a thousand-things-to-do. We can resist this disease, but only with the proper inoculations.[64]

The first step is to recognise, name, and resist the forces around us that work against our pursuit of spiritual leisure or a contemplative life. But changing the externals won't be enough. Many women and some men have left their fast-paced, high-pressure work in the professional world to be home with their young children, expecting in their new life to have time for quiet, prayer, and contemplation. Often they find that the pace of their life hasn't changed at all, and finding quiet is just as difficult as before, if not more so. The most critical change, it turns out, is within, in our attitudes, assumptions, habits, patterns, and expectations.[65]

We sometimes feel and act as if we're victims of time, the passive subjects of forces totally outside our control. But time is not something that happens to us. We can make choices about how we live our lives, more often than we may think, and as we make them we discover that new possibilities open up. To make these against-the-grain choices, however, will require that we give up something, that we spurn societal definitions and affirmations of success, that we redefine and be satisfied with 'enough'. All that is possible only when our life is firmly grounded in contemplation. As we begin to nurture and cultivate our own spirituality of leisure, we will begin also to see why that is fundamental to living well. 'The grace that abounds will be its own reward.'[66]

At a glance

Living more fully means tuning into the world around us.

We need to 'be' before we 'do'.

Children can teach us everything about living in the moment.

CHAPTER SIX

Clearing the decks

DROWNING IN INFORMATION

We are living in a world that has gone information crazy. We have coming at us from every direction every moment of the day a huge amount of information. To loosely paraphrase the late Sir Winston Churchill, 'Never before in human history have people been subjected to such an unrelenting torrent of information and data coming at them from so many angles and at such speed.' In fact what we are drowning in is data, not information. To call it information implies that we have the capacity to understand, absorb and process it. But, it's coming at us so fast that we often feel we're drowning in it. We can't take it in. There's simply too much of it to be processed. Doctors have become aware of a new syndrome called Information Fatigue Syndrome. The symptoms include paralysis of analytical ability, mounting anxiety and self-doubt and an increasing tendency to blame others.

It has been suggested that more than one-third of all reported stress-related illnesses are being caused by information overload. I recently did a search on the Internet for a certain phrase and ended up with 27,000 separate references! We have a great thirst for more information, especially the new, but we lack the ability or the time to make use of it. It is almost as if Western people are searching for the missing key to human existence in an ever-increasing torrent of information, perhaps even searching for salvation. We feel that there is something missing in our lives, despite our material well-being, and we are seeking the answer in more and more information. But it is an illusion. We will not find the answers to life in more information, no matter how clever and sophisticated the information may be.

LEARNED HELPLESSNESS

We live in a cynical and jaundiced age. Many people have watched their hopes and dreams evaporate in the avalanche of violence and confusion. However, if we are to build a more caring world we need to regain a vision for our society and for ourselves. In the ABC TV series *Wildside*, former policeman Bill McCoy has befriended two street kids, Joe and Heidi, while hunting for his missing son. They've both become enmeshed in a web of crime, drugs and sexual abuse. In a powerful and moving scene McCoy says to them, 'The only hope we've got is a few screwed-up people caring about each other.' 'What screwed-up people?' asks Joe. 'You, Heidi, me — if we care about each other we've got hope', says McCoy. 'Bullshit,' is Heidi's terse response. Within a few hours she is dead in a ram raid on a shop and we're tempted to believe she is right. In a sense she is, unless we begin to care about each other. There is no hope for the world unless we put aside our protective mechanisms, and care about other human beings.[67]

At times like the Port Arthur and Thredbo tragedies we see the best come out in us as people genuinely care for each other. But we need to begin to draw on that reservoir of care and compassion that I believe is there in most people I know — to care for each other in the ordinary struggles of life, not just wait for the tragedies of life. We may be screwed up, to use Bill McCoy's language, but unless we begin to look out for each other in new ways there is no hope for our society.

CONDITIONED HELPLESSNESS

Heidi's attitude to life is a classic case of what psychologist Martin Seligman calls 'learned helplessness'. Heidi has allowed herself to be conditioned by life's experiences to believe that no-one cares about her and that things will always end badly. Often this kind of conditioning begins very early in life. Seligman discovered 'learned helplessness' as a result of a controlled experiment with a group of dogs to test the theory that emotional learning could transfer across widely different situations. Over a period of some weeks the dogs had been exposed to high-pitched tones and brief shocks. The tones and the shocks were given to the dogs in pairs – first a tone and then a shock. The shocks were quite mild, more like static electricity, the aim being to get the dogs to associate the neutral tone and the noxious shock, so that later when they heard the tone they would react to it with fear as if it were a shock. Then the dogs were put in a large box divided by a low wall into two compartments. The investigators wanted to see if the dogs in the box would react to the tone in the same way they had learned to react to the shock — by jumping the barrier to get away. To escape the shock all they had to do was to jump over the low barrier, something dogs usually learn easily. However, instead of jumping the barrier to escape the shocks the dogs just lay there whimpering.[68] Seligman realised that because during their conditioning nothing the dogs did could stop the shocks they had simply given up. They had come to the conclusion or 'learned' that nothing mattered. This is what is known as 'learned helplessness'.

FLEAS WITH SORE HEADS

The story is told of a man who had a jar of fleas. He initially kept a lid on the jar so when the fleas jumped up to escape from the jar they hit their heads on the lid. Finally he removed the lid, but the fleas had learned from experience that it was not possible to jump higher than the lid and that is exactly what they would do — jump to the height of the lid, but no further. The story is also told of the cat that jumped on a hotplate when it was on. It never did it again. In fact, it never went anywhere near a stove for the rest of its life. Our conditioning can cause us to have certain expectations of life and these expectations can limit what we achieve. We see this principle operating in society all the time, at school when students try and try and try, but fail and finally give up, convinced that no matter how hard they try they can never succeed. They believe the odds are against them. We also see it among the ranks of the unemployed. When someone has applied again and again for jobs and is continually knocked back, or more often doesn't even get an interview, they give up because they believe they have no chance of getting a job. Only when we are valued or can value ourselves for who we are, rather than what we do or achieve, can we have a real sense of self worth.

UNCLUTTERING OUR LIVES

Most people I know want to live simpler lives. They feel their lives are too cluttered up with things. Advertisers constantly bombard us with propaganda that we need to buy this or that gadget to save time. But most people find these gadgets simply make more work. The more gadgets you have the greater the chance of one of them breaking down. Entire institutions can be paralysed if the computer system goes down. I'm not joking. Haven't you been in a bank when the computers are down? Did anyone ever ask us if we wanted the new technology? Were we given time to reflect on whether we felt it would improve our lives overall or the kind of society we live in? Or was it simply introduced by those who wanted to make money from it? Certainly computers have made many more things possible, but learning how to do those things and actually doing them takes a great deal more time. The new technology has made business and industry more efficient but has it improved the quality of our lives? There are fewer jobs than ever before because the technology can do them. Car factories that used to be worker intensive can now be run by just a few technicians. The result is huge numbers of people out of work. We can talk to each on mobile phones and see each other on TV phones. We can experience colour stereo TV and surf the Net to our 'greedy for new things' heart's content but does it improve our ability to communicate with one another as human beings? Does it strengthen and deepen our already weakened sense of community? Or does it do the opposite?

INHABITING OUR INNER SPACE

In a world of endless noise and frenetic busyness silence becomes even more precious. I find myself these days increasingly turning away from the avalanche of information that seeks to invade my mind at every opportunity, to make safe, quiet spaces in the day, and the night. It doesn't have to be long, but it does have to be long enough to relax and focus. I am making more time to meditate on the Scriptures. When I first began to pray in a contemplative way it was quite scary. I found that when I spent any time in quietness all that happened was that I remembered all the things I had to do. A whole range of thoughts invaded my consciousness and prevented me from being still. One of the first things I did was to keep a pad and pen beside me during these times so I could write down the jobs as they popped into my mind. Some friends gave me an electronic organiser and I discovered that was an effective tool to record these persistent interruptions to my attempts at stillness.

Then I learned to do some simple exercises to relax my body before beginning to pray. I imagine all the different muscles of my body tensing and then relaxing. I start with my head and work down to my toes. I have known for most of my adult life that prayer is a good thing to do. But, I have struggled to do it consistently, because I am very much a doer. Yet, when I pray not only does God hear and answer my prayers — not always I might add in the way I would like — but I also benefit from the act of praying. Being still is good for us. We have been designed to spend times of quiet and reflection in between the activity. I find not only do I hear more clearly what God is saying to me, but also praying changes my perspective. Often the things that seemed important, the things that needed urgent doing, recede into the background.

INNER SOLITUDE

We need to take time off from business to be still and listen to our own voice and the voice of God. In our busy world it is not easy to do. Charles Ringma suggests we need to find a 'new centre of inner quietness and certitude from which we act in the midst of a busy and demanding world'.[69] If I've taken time to achieve that inner quiet my day proves far more productive and I'm able to react in a far more Christ-like way to the stresses and tensions of the day. The solitude enables me to appropriate the fruit of the Spirit of God in my life. Many people are afraid of being silent for any period of time. Often we are scared of what we might learn about ourselves in the silence so we run away from ever being alone. If we never take the time to be still enough to listen to our own many voices how can we expect to hear God's voice? Charles Ringma asserts:

> In our much doing we lose perspective, lose our energy and more importantly lose our creativity and sense of humour. And there is nothing more severe or boring than a humourless person. We can through over-doing, begin to carry the world on our own shoulders and become overwhelmed, disillusioned and even burnt-out.[70]

Fasting is an increasingly popular practice, for both spiritual and health purposes. In our noise-filled world fasting from words for a period of time is a very productive thing to do. It can help us to realise that much of what we say isn't all that important. It enables us to reflect more on what life is all about.

GETTING OUR PRIORITIES RIGHT

After my son died I came to see that there is only one thing that is really important in this world — loving relationships. For me this means a loving relationship with God and my family, church family and friends. If we lose our possessions, our jobs, our homes, even our health we can keep on living. But if we lose those relationships we've lost the most precious thing in life. One of the best-known books on prayer in the Christian tradition was written by a seventeenth century monk called Brother Lawrence. Brother Lawrence was a cook who learned that the ordinary events of daily life can be times of prayer as much as saying prayers or going to church.

In fact, Brother Lawrence claimed he felt closer to God in his daily work than he did during special times of prayer and devotion: 'We can do little things for God; I turn the cake that is frying on the pan for love of him — It is enough for me to pick up but a straw from the ground for the love of God.'[71]

Often, religious people make too sharp a distinction between prayer and life. However, if, like Brother Lawrence, we see prayer and living as one and the same thing all of life can become prayer. Prayer is living in a constant state of awareness of God's presence. There is never a moment when God is not with us. Why do we sometimes act as if God's not here? Some years ago in an effort to remind myself of God's constant presence during the day I decided that every time I opened a door I would remind myself that God was with me — to make opening the door a prayer. It worked.

SET YOUR OWN AGENDA

In the first year of our married life a wise friend advised us, 'Set your own agenda for your life together because if you don't others will set it for you.' His words proved to be prophetic. We've been struggling to set our own agenda ever since. I know that some people hate setting goals. It feels to them like hell on Earth to have to sit down and think through where they want their lives to head. They'd rather hang loose and just let life happen. But someone once said that if you aim for nothing that's exactly what you'll get. There's a wonderful scene in *Alice in Wonderland* when Alice is lost and asking which road she should take. The Mad Hatter asks her where she wants to go and she replies that it doesn't really matter. 'Then,' he says, 'it doesn't really matter which road you take.'

In his book *First Things First* Stephen Covey suggests that we should always begin with the end in mind. Covey asks, 'How many people on their deathbed wish they had spent more time at the office?'[72] We could add, 'How many people at the end of their lives wish they'd spent more time doing dishes or cleaning the house?' He has devised a very useful exercise to help people develop some specific goals in life. He suggests that we create in our minds a picture of our eightieth birthday party and imagine the speeches given in our honour on that occasion and listen to all that is said about the kind of life we lived. Then having heard what has been said he suggests we sit down and write out our goals for the rest of our life. This is a helpful way of deciding how we want to spend the rest of our lives.

For those of you who have an aversion to high-powered business management techniques let me put it another way, 'Show me your hopes and your dreams and I'll show you your future.' Some people feel pressured by the thought of putting down their dreams on paper. However, there is something very helpful about the process of writing. When you write down your hopes it makes you think through what is and isn't really important to you. In the process you may well discover that some of the things you really wanted to do aren't all that important. And in the reflective process you may become aware of other things that you want to do. There may appear to be a contradiction in my suggesting that we need to set goals for the future at the same time as learning to live more effectively in the moment. However, the purpose for setting the goals and establishing our priorities is to free us to live more in the moment. I should say though that I've discovered that the more I want to do the less time I have and the more complicated life becomes. I suspect that the only way to live simpler lives is to want less.

RESETTING OUR PRIORITIES

Often at a funeral service I encourage those present to take time to reflect on their lives. I ask them to consider what epitaph will be placed on their grave when they die and how they are planning to live the rest of their life in a way that really counts. Educationist, James Fowler draws up a list of questions that are helpful in resetting our life's agenda. He asks:

- What are you spending and being spent for? What commands and receives your best time and energy?
- What goals, dreams or institutions are you pouring out your life for?
- As you live your life what power or powers do you fear or dread? What power or powers do you rely on or trust?
- To what or to whom are you committed in life? In death?
- With whom or with what group do you share your most sacred or private hopes for life and for the lives of those who love you?
- What are those most sacred and compelling hopes and purposes in your life?[73]

At a glance

We can set our own agenda.

Changing our priorities is the first step to a
fuller more meaningful life.

Being aware and living more simply can
help us live more fully.

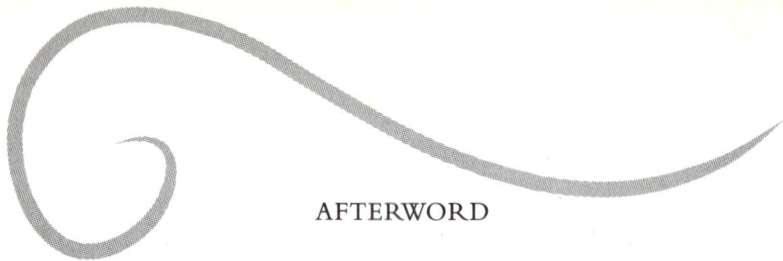

AFTERWORD

Having suggested a number of ways to live more fully in the moment I need to say that, while what I've offered to you can help you live life more fully in the moment, my ability to live in the present is inextricably linked to my faith in Jesus Christ. For me faith in Christ, and the belief that life goes on beyond death for all who put their trust in him, is what frees me to live more completely now. Malcom Muggeridge once said that the greatest tragedy of life is to come to believe that this world is our home; that this is all there is. I love life on this planet. I love being a husband and a father and a priest. I enjoy each day, with all its joys and struggles. Life is good. But, I know that life here will one day end. Because, with Malcom Muggeridge and millions of other Christians, I believe that this life is not all there is, life takes on a different perspective. As Henri Nouwen expressed it so well:

God is a God of the present. God is always in the moment, be that moment hard or easy, joyful or painful. When Jesus spoke about God, he always spoke about God as being where and when we are. 'When you see me you see God. When you hear me you hear God.' God is not someone who was or will be, but the One who is, and who is for me in the present moment. That's why Jesus came to wipe away the burdens of the past and the worries for the future. He wants us to discover God right where we are, here and now.[74]

For me, life on this Earth is just a beginning, albeit a very wonderful beginning, but not an end in itself. Ultimately my security in life is in a relationship with Christ, not the money I have in the bank or my possessions, or even in my wife and family. Having Jesus Christ at the centre of my life and knowing that life on this Earth is only the beginning enables me to live more fully here and now. My relationship with Christ frees me to more fully become the person God created me to be. I trust the Lord with the whole of my life, whether I live to be one hundred or whether I die tomorrow.

REFERENCES

Chapter One — The dilemma

[1]Chapin, Harry, 'Cat's in the Cradle'.

[2]Hammarskjöld, Dag, *Markings*, translated by W.H. Auden and Leif Sjoberg, London: Faber and Faber, 1964, p.37.

[3]Quoted by Kennon Callahan in *Effective Church Leadership*, New York: Harper and Row, 1990, pp. 101–102.

[4]Taken from *Here and Now: Living in the Spirit*, London: published and copyright Darton, Longman and Todd Limited, 1994, p.4. Used by permission of the publishers.

[5]Ibid.

[6]Quoted in article 'Stressed workers seek job changes' by Alan Thornhill in *The West Australian*, 31st December 1997, p. 1.

[7]From a private journal.

[8]Campolo, Tony, *Carpe Diem — Seize the Day*, Dallas: Word Publishing, 1994, pp. 13–15.

[9]Sansom, Clive, *The Witnesses and Other Poems*, London: Methuen, 1965, p. 74.

[10]Arnott, Paul, *No Time To Say Goodbye*, Sydney: Albatross Books, 1992, p. 81.

Chapter Two — People who have learned to live in the moment

[11]General Editor, Kenneth Barker; *The Holy Bible*, *The New International Version Study Bible*, Grand Rapids: Zondervan, 1985, p. 1452.

[12]Ibid.

[13]Ibid.

[14]Ibid.

[15]Ibid.

[16]Ibid.

[17]Ibid.

[18]From the film *Gone With The Wind*.

[19]Editor Kenneth Taylor; *The Living Bible*, London: Hodder & Stoughton and Coverdale House Publishers, 1972, p. 1345.

[20]I asked Margaret Houston to write this. Margaret is a columnist for *Alive* magazine.

[21]Joanne Cornish (née Dick) is a friend, whom I interviewed specifically for this book.

[22]The Banham family belonged to Camp Quality and I interviewed them especially for *Live the Moment*.

[23]I interviewed Peter Crosswell for this book.

Chapter Three — Dealing with the past

[24]Dobson, Theodore Elliot, *Inner Healing: God's Great Assurance,* New York: Paulist Press, 1978, p. 125.

[25]Linn, Matthew and Dennis, *Healing Life's Hurts*, New York: Paulist Press, 1978, p. 11.

[26]MacNutt, Francis, *The Power To Heal,* Ave Maria Press, 1977, p. 39.

[27]*Holy Bible, NIV Study Bible*, pp. 932–33.

[28]Taken from Buckley, Michael, *Do Not Be Afraid*, London: published and copyright Darton, Longman and Todd, 1995, pp. 115–16. Used by permission of the publishers.

[29]Ibid., p. 117.

[30]Ibid.

[31]Sanford, John A., *Healing and Wholeness*, New York: Paulist Press, 1977, p.29.

[32]Comment in a letter to me by Cathy Ann Matthews, the author of *Breaking Through* (Sutherland: Albatross Books, 1990).

[33]Pytches, Mary, *Yesterday's Child*, Hodder & Stoughton, 1990, p. 11.

[34]Ibid., p. 19.

[35]Ibid.

[36]Ibid., pp. 22–23.

References

[37]I heard Fr Francis MacNutt tell this story at a conference in Sydney in 1979.

[38]*Holy Bible, NIV Study Bible*, p. 1586.

[39]Allender, Dan, *The Wounded Heart*, North Geelong: CWR, 1992, p. 18.

[40]Dowrick, Stephanie, *Forgiveness and Other Acts of Love*, Ringwood: Viking, 1997, pp. 289–290.

[41]Ibid., p. 291.

[42]Carter-Stapleton, Ruth, *The Experience of Inner Healing*, London: Hodder & Stoughton, 1978, pp. 62–63.

[43]Andrews, Magaret, 'How Our Families Shape Us', article published in *Threshold Magazine* — a magazine about marriage education (1996) Vol. 53, No. 24.

[44]Ibid.

[45]Ibid.

Chapter Four — Facing the future

[46]Eds Gabrielle Carey and Rosemary Sorensen, *The Penguin Book of Death*, Ringwood: Penguin Books, 1997.

[47]Peck, M. Scott, *Further Along the Road Less Travelled*, New York: Simon and Schuster, 1993, p. 48.

[48]Ibid., p. 49.

[49]Ibid., pp. 49–50.

[50]Nouwen, Henri J.M., *Beyond The Mirror*, London: Fount Paperbacks, 1990, p. 33.

[51]Ibid., pp. 33–34.

[52]De Mello, Anthony, *Sadhana, a way to God*, Anand: Gujarat Sahitya Prakash, 1988, pp. 109–110.

[53]Carnegie, Dale, *How To Stop Worrying And Start Living*, Kingswood: World's Work Ltd, 1977, p. 22.

[54]Ibid., p. 23.

[55]Peck, M. Scott, *The Road Less Travelled*, London: Rider, 1988, p. 15.

Chapter Five — Tuning in to the present

[56]Rice, Jim, 'Why Play?', article in *Sojourners Online*, January–February, 1997, Vol. 26, No. 1.

[57]De Mello, Anthony, *Sadhana, a way to God*, Anand: Gujarat Sahitya Prakash, 1988, pp. 7–8.

[58]Ibid., p. 9.

[59]Kahn, Albert E., *Joys and Sorrows: Reflections by Pablo Casals*, London: Macdonald and Co. Ltd., 1970.

[60]Grant, Peter. This was written on request for this book.

[61]Sansom, Clive, *The Witnesses*, p. 27.

[62]Rice, op. cit., p. 3.

[63]Ibid., pp. 3–4

[64]Ibid., p. 4.

[65]Ibid.

[66]Ibid.

Chapter Six — Clearing the decks

[67]From the first series of the ABC TV program *Wildside*.

[68]Seligman, Martin E.P., *Learned Optimism*, Sydney: Random House, 1993, pp. 19–20.

[69]Ringma, Charles, *Dare to Journey*, Sydney: Albatross Books, 1992 from 'Reflection 7'.

[70]Ibid.

[71]*The Spiritual Maxims of Brother Lawrence*, Westwood: Fleming H Revell, 1967, pp. 36–37.

[72]Covey, Stephen R., and Merrill, A. Roger, *First Things First*, New York: Simon and Schuster, 1994, p. 17.

[73]Fowler, J., *Stages of Faith*, Blackburn: Dove Communications, 1981, p. 3.

Afterword

[74]Nouwen, Henri, op. cit., pp. 4–5.